TEACHING THE WRITING PROCESS IN HIGH SCHOOL

Standards Consensus Series

National Council of Teachers of English
1111 W. Kenyon Road, Urbana, Illinois 61801-1096

Production Editor: Jamie Hutchinson

Series Cover Design and Interior Design: Joellen Bryant

NCTE Stock Number 52864-3050

Library of Congress Cataloging-in-Publication Data

Teaching the writing process in high school.
     p.   cm. — (Standards consensus series)
  ISBN 0-8141-5286-4 (pbk.)
  1. English language—Composition and exercises—Study and teaching (Secondary)—United States. I. National Council of Teachers of English. II. Series.
  LB1631.T29 1995
  808'.042'0712—dc20   95-40688
                                      CIP

CONTENTS

3. Emphasis: Peer Editing, Self Editing, Revision

INTRODUCTION

RATIONALE FOR THE STANDARDS CONSENSUS SERIES

Much attention is given to matters that divide the teaching profession. But when NCTE collected dozens of standards statements, curriculum frameworks, and other key state curriculum documents in order to prepare *State of the States—A Report on English Language Arts Content Standards in Each State,* considerable agreement was evident in many areas of English language arts instruction. Similar consensus has been demonstrated in the development of *The NCTE/IRA Standards for the English Language Arts,* the core document that outlines national standards in our discipline.

A heartening fact has emerged from the standards movement, as varied as that movement has been: We are after all a community of teachers who draw upon shared instructional traditions in literature, composition, language, and related areas. Furthermore, in recent years the insight and invention of teachers and teacher educators have built upon those traditions in fascinating ways. The result is a rich body of practice-oriented material that parallels the mounting consensus in the profession.

NCTE has developed the Standards Consensus Series, then, in recognition of the existence of core beliefs about the English language arts as revealed in innumerable standards-related documents and classroom ideas generated by teachers. The assumption underlying the series—and illustrated in it—is that good teachers have long been carrying out English language arts programs and classroom activities that exemplify sound implementation of the commonly held standards. The contents of each volume in the Standards Consensus Series were selected mainly from a database of classroom-practice materials. The database materials had been selected by teachers from a larger body of writings previously published by NCTE, mainly in the popular *NOTES Plus* journal.

Between the covers of this volume you will find some of the most exciting of the classroom experiences that deal with one major area of consensus in the profession—*Teaching the Writing Process in High School.* Below is a sampling of statements from various standards documents that testify to our common belief in the teaching and learning of many aspects of the writing process:

Ohio—Students become aware that writing is a means of clarifying thinking and that it is a process which embodies several stages, including prewriting, drafting, receiving responses, revising, editing, and postwriting activities, including evaluation. (10)

Alaska—Students will speak and write well for a variety of purposes and audiences . . . revise, edit, and publish their own writing as appropriate . . . evaluate their own speaking and writing and that of others, using high standards. (n.p.)

North Dakota—The students actively engage in the writing process. . . . use planning to organize thoughts before writing . . . understand that composing a piece may require drafts to reflect the author's purpose and thoughts . . . use feedback to revise . . . edit to improve comprehension. (31)

Arkansas—Students will use writing as a means of exploring thought and as a process involving prewriting activities, drafting, receiving feedback, revising, editing, and postwriting activities, including evaluating, publishing and displaying. (1)

Indiana—Students understand the process of writing and know a variety of strategies to: organize and generate ideas; write a draft; rethink and revise content as appropriate for audience and purpose; improve writing based on peer and teacher response; edit and proofread for grammar, word usage, mechanics, and spelling; and use dictionaries and handbooks for revising and editing. (n.p.)

Utah—Students write a variety of texts, using the processes and elements of writing. . . . (n.p.)

Delaware—Using the processes of effective readers, writers, listeners, viewers, and speakers, [students] will be able to . . . use written and oral English appropriate for various purposes and audiences. (8)

South Carolina--Students use language processes and strategies effectively to communicate. . . . Students should employ various strategies and processes. . . . The more students know and can articulate these processes and strategies, the better they will be able to use them in any situation or context. (14)

Colorado--Students write and speak for a variety of purposes and for diverse audiences, . . . selecting a focused topic and drafting, revising, editing, and proofreading a final copy for a larger audience. (5, 6)

Massachusetts—Effective communicators . . . construct and convey meaning through the processes of reading, writing, speak
ing, listening, viewing, and presenting. They understand reading, writing, speaking, listening, viewing, and presenting as
communication processes. (39)

These varied and powerful expressions of belief in the importance
of writing point to the usefulness of this collection of materials as a key
volume in the Standards Consensus Series. Of course, this is not to suggest that this book is of value only to those seeking to establish relationships between standards and instructional practice. Every high school
teacher of English language arts will find a wealth of lively, academically
well-grounded ideas in this volume. Even if there had been no "standards movement" as such, these materials would nonetheless present a
profile of exemplary practice worthy of emulation in improving students'
performance in the English language arts.

A few comments are in order about the nature of the materials and
their organization. Consistent with NCTE position statements and with
the texts of many standards documents, most of the classroom practices
here do not isolate the teaching of writing as if it were unrelated to the
entire range of English language arts skills and topics. The materials in
the Standards Consensus Series demonstrate amply that good teachers
often do everything at once—asking students to reflect on and talk about
literary experiences, encouraging them to make notes about their readings and discussions in preparation for writing, and finding other ways
to weave the language arts together in an integral learning experience.

A North Carolina goals document makes this point especially well:
"Communication is an interactive process that brings together the
communicator(s), the activity or task, and the situation that surrounds
them. It is a constructive, dynamic process, not an isolated event or an
assembly of a set of sub-skills. . . . Though listed separately, the [North
Carolina] goals are not to be perceived as linear or isolated entities. The
goals are interrelated aspects of the dynamic process of communication"
(46). While the focus of this volume is mainly on teaching the writing
process, then, these classroom experiences typically exemplify the dy-
namics of real teaching.

ORGANIZATION OF THIS BOOK

The materials in *Teaching the Writing Process in High School* are grouped in
useful ways that will be described below. However, neither the details of
a particular classroom experience nor the arrangement of materials in
this text is intended to be prescriptive. The day of know-all, tell-all books
is past. Student populations differ; cookie-cutter activities simply don't
work in every classroom environment. Most significant, teachers know
their own students and have sound intuitions about the kinds of ideas
and materials that are and are not appropriate in their classrooms. From
this solid collection of materials, teachers are invited to select, discard,

amplify, adapt, and integrate ideas in light of the students they work with and know.

The organization of this book does, though, provide a strong conception of teaching the writing process and some useful pathways for appropriate classroom practice. An underlying assumption is that writing process instruction is *a teaching model* that makes use of our understanding of how real-world composing is carried out. No teaching model can wholly codify or duplicate the complex and varied psychological processes of composing; but a model can reflect and emulate those processes. Good teachers build key aspects of the writing process into instruction even while acknowledging individualized patterns of learning among their students and striving to remain open to the essentially fluid, recursive nature of composing.

The various state standards documents and the body of teaching practices that were reviewed in compiling this volume were powerfully suggestive of ways of organizing the text. Two pervasive aspects of writing process instruction—audience and purpose--were interwoven with other aspects of process instruction in most of the classroom experiences described by teachers. But certain activities emphasized audience and purpose, and these are included in **Section 1—Emphasis: Audience and Purpose.**

Jackie Proett and Kent Gill state in *The Writing Process in Action,* "The audience for any writing activity can be designated as part of the assignment or it can exist naturally in the writing situation; it can be simulated or real" (13). Section 1 begins with five classroom activities that involve follow-through to real audiences. These are followed by activities that deal with simulated audiences, often focusing on how the "same" message can be cast differently for various audiences. The three final entries furnish a neat transition to the next section. Besides highlighting audience and purpose, they focus on the topic of **Section 2—Emphasis: Prewriting and Drafting.** In practice, these two components of writing process instruction are typically paired, since virtually all prewriting activities culminate in an initial draft, which benefits from the prewriting activities.

The repertoire of prewriting strategies used by teachers in Section 2 is quite broad. It includes brainstorming, small- and large-group discussion, interviews, freewrites, introspection, field trips, visuals and music, and numerous other methods. After a useful overview in the opening entry, "Prewriting as Motivation," the focus is on prewriting ideas that draw on the student's personal experiences and imagination. Then, beginning with "Raiders of the Lost Art of Storytelling," several items combine experiential prewriting with reading or writing in a variety of literary forms. Literature takes on increasing prominence toward the end of the section, where the prewriting activities lead to writing, reading, and/ or viewing in forms that include short stories, novels, poems, and even popular media such as newspapers and films.

This section underlines a point raised earlier—that creative teachers do not segment the language arts or regard the writing process as a series of isolated steps. For example, the last four entries in Section 2 link written and oral language instruction with short stories, films, protest-song lyrics, and newspapers. While emphasizing prewriting, the items all suggest follow-throughs that deal in varying degrees with drafting, editing, revising, and publishing.

In **Section 3—Emphasis: Peer Editing, Self Editing, Revision,** titles such as "Constructive Feedback," "Students Take Ownership of Their Reports," and "Keeping Student Critics Honest" demonstrate how far the profession has come since the days of error-oriented pedagogy and red-pencil assaults on students' texts. The teachers here are clearly committed to having students discuss one another's work as a community of writers and to helping students internalize principles of critical response so they can carry their critiquing skills beyond the classroom. The first ten entries typically involve students in responding to insight-generating questions about their writings. There is remarkable ingenuity and variety in the way teachers set up critical interaction and self-assessment--from individual introspection to dyads to small groups to whole-class discussion; from generic questions to assignment-specific ones; from experiential to literature-based writings. Teachers today are furnishing numerous models for helping students to become more independent writer-learners. The rest of Section 3 suggests many ways of broadening and enlivening self-assessment and peer evaluation. Student editorial boards and proofreading groups, turn-taking and clustering, role-assignment in the critiquing process, self-identification of problems, and the use of students as specialist-tutors are but a few of the inventive ideas.

In a time of considerable pessimism and discord in education, it is encouraging to find major grounds for consensus in the teaching of the English language arts. In state and national standards statements that are being developed throughout the country, we find *common goals* for the teaching of our discipline. In the reported practices of the English language arts teaching community, we find *a formidable body of ideas about how to achieve those goals.* The Standards Consensus Series is both a recognition of cohesiveness and a tool for growth in the profession.

Finally, some acknowledgments are in order. First, kudos to the teachers and teacher educators who contributed their thoughtful practices to this collection, mostly via past issues of NCTE's *NOTES Plus.* The texts from that periodical are virtually unchanged, and the institutional affiliations of the teachers reflect their teaching assignments at the time of original publication. Issues of *NOTES Plus* and many other high school publications have been regularly reviewed by chairs of the NCTE Secondary Section. These include the present chair, Joan Naomi Steiner, and former chairs Mildred Miller, Jackie Swensson, Faith Schullstrom, George B. Shea, Jr., Theodore Hipple, and Skip Nicholson. Staff coordinators and advisors for *NOTES Plus* have also been a key in this endeavor. The staff coordinator since 1985 has been Felice Kaufmann. The teachers who categorized the vast body of materials for inclusion in NCTE's general database of teaching practices are Carol Snyder and Jim Forman. This text was compiled by Charles Suhor, NCTE Deputy Executive Director.

REFERENCES

Alaska Department of Education. 1994. *Alaska Student Performance Standards.*

Arkansas Department of Education. 1993. *Arkansas English Language Arts Curriculum Framework.*

[Colorado] Standards and Assessment Council. December 1994. *Model Content Standards for Reading, Writing, Mathematics, Science, History, and Geography.* Final discussion draft.

Delaware Department of Public Instruction. 1995. *English Language Arts Content Standards.* Document Control #95-01/94/10/08.

Essential Skills Content Standards for Language Arts and Mathematics [Indiana]. 1993. Published in *Indiana Educator,* Spring 1994.

Massachusetts Department of Education. March 1995. *English Language Arts Curriculum Content Chapter: Constructing and Conveying Meaning.* Draft.

North Carolina Department of Public Instruction. 1992. *Competency-Based Curriculum. Teacher Handbook: Communication Skills, K–12.*

North Dakota Department of Public Instruction. 1994. *English Language Arts Curriculum Frameworks: Standards and Benchmarks.*

Ohio Department of Education, Division of Curriculum, Instruction, and Professional Development. 1992. *Model Competency-Based Language Arts Program.*

Proett, Jackie, and Kent Gill. 1986. *The Writing Process in Action: A Handbook for Teachers.* Urbana, IL: NCTE, 1986.

South Carolina English Language Arts Curriculum Framework Writing Team. February 1995. *English Language Arts Framework.* Field review draft.

Utah State Office of Education. February 1995. *Standards for Utah, K-6.*

1 | EMPHASIS: AUDIENCE AND PURPOSE

| WRITING FOR KIDS

One of the most successful projects in my junior and senior creative-writing class is the creation of a storybook for elementary students. The germ of this idea came from a colleague, who had used a somewhat simpler version of the same project.

The goal is for each student to interview the grade-school student for whom the book is intended, write the story, illustrate the work, create a title page with publishing information and an author's page, and, finally, compile all the pages inside an attractive cover.

In my introduction to this project, I explain to my students that we'll be taking a field trip to a nearby third-grade classroom, where each student writer will interview one third-grader. Prior to the trip, I contact the grade-school teacher and get a printout of the youngsters' names. I ask my students each to choose one of the names and prepare at least twenty interview questions that could spark ideas for a story. As a class, we talk about possible topics for questions—the third grader's hobbies, activities, names of pets and friends, and other interesting facts.

After my students have chosen names from the printout, we warm up to the task of writing interview questions by remembering some of our own third-grade interests, hobbies, and pets. Talking and jotting down a few details helps put students in the right frame of mind for questioning their third-grade partners.

On the day I've arranged for my students to visit the grade school for the interviews, the third-graders are looking forward to the visit as much as the high school students are. The eight-year-olds delight in having the older students visit, ask questions, and take an avid interest in them.

After the interviews are completed, I take a picture of each pair of students—"interviewer" and "interviewee." Each third-grader chooses the exact place on the playground to have the picture taken. This picture will be used on the "author's page" of the storybook.

After being with the third-graders for about an hour and a half, my student writers return to high school to begin work on the book. Using the interview notes and conferring as needed, the writers create stories that they think the younger students will find interesting. For example, Gina, a third-grader, said that she liked tap dancing and wanted to be a dancer; she even left her seat during her interview to demonstrate her tap dancing skills. In response, the high school student who interviewed her wrote a story about a young girl who tried to get her "big break" in show business in New York, was discovered, and then hired to be on a weekly television show.

After the story has been written, the writer may want to meet with a peer for feedback. After making revisions on the story, the writer must also create the cover; the title page, which includes the publishing information; and the author's page, which includes a brief biographical sketch and the photo taken on the playground. This personalized approach makes the finished books mean all the more to their recipients.

When my students are ready, we spend a class period at the grade school, personally delivering the books. The third-grade students have anticipated this moment for almost a month, and are always excited to receive the finished products. I take one final group picture: my creative writing students standing with the third-graders, who are proudly holding their books. This keepsake is a fitting tribute to a project one senior called the "highlight" of the entire creative writing unit.

Mary Philip, Belleville Township High School East, Belleville, Illinois

Special Pen Pals

A GENERATION GAP NARROWS

Another head peered into my classroom while I was attempting to wolf down a tuna sandwich during my lunch break. "Would you pass this on to Mrs. Miller? I wrote this letter to her. It's three pages!"

"Great!" I said. "I'll run over to the nursing home this afternoon."

That was another one of my reluctant writers, now a little less reluctant.

Other bodies appeared at my door between classes, during homeroom, or during their lunch periods. "Do you have any letters for us?"

"Did you hear anything from Mr. Robinson yet? I asked him all sorts of questions in my last letter. I made my dad drop it off on his way to work the other day."

I teach basic writing classes at Blue Mountain Middle School and Hendrick Hudson High School in Montrose, New York. Students are placed in my program if they are identified as being one or more years below grade level in basic writing skills. Most of these students hate school and hate to write; to compound the situation, they are taken out of their physical education classes twice a week to attend my program. Not surprisingly, many of them would rather be tossing a ball around than sitting at a desk with pen and notebook. On arriving, students typically complained, "I know how to write good already!" "Do I have to come to this?" "Could I get a note from my mother saying it's okay to go back to gym?"

To win these kids over, I had to make writing exciting, useful, and worthwhile. And only then, after getting students to want to write, could I help make them better writers.

I wanted my students to feel they were writing for a significant audience. Matching kids with pen pals who have common interests seemed like a logical idea. But pen pals who lived far away, whom my students would most likely never get to meet, would not generate the long-term enthusiasm I wanted. Pen pals who lived nearby and who were not much different from my students' current friends would not light that spark either. The solution that came to me was a pen-pal project that would cross the generation gap.

I called the director of a nursing home in a nearby community, who was delighted to participate in the project. The senior citizens involved would have a chance to make new friends and to share their problems and concerns as well as all their years of life experience. They would again be in touch with the outside world from a very young point of view. My students would make friends too and would have interested audiences for their writing.

The project was presented to both groups as a community service. The nursing home residents would have a chance to befriend youngsters who were academically weak and disliked school; my basic writing students would have an opportunity to cheer up senior citizens who were sick or unable to take care of themselves, who were lonely, and whose lives were nearing their end. Both groups were intrigued by the idea.

After I taught my students proper business-letter form, I asked them to write pen-pal-request letters to the nursing home describing their interests and hobbies and the kind of pen pal each would prefer.

The nursing home did the rest. An avid boy scout was matched up with a former boy scout leader. A baseball enthusiast was matched up with a woman whose grandson played on a professional team. A teenager who formerly lived in Ireland was matched up with a very Irish grandmother who frequently visited Ireland.

A student who hunted stated in his pen-pal-request letter: "I would like you to match me up with a man who also likes to hunt," and mumbled under his breath, "I bet none of those old fogies do that!" But upon reading his first letter, a two-page account of a senior's hunting exploits, the student's eyes lit up, and he immediately began writing a long letter back, filled with his own hunting experiences.

Prewriting activities for the project included discussions about what it must be like to be old and about students' relationships with their own grandparents. Students also filled out interest inventories for use in their initial request letters and wrote futuristic stories on the topic, "My Life in the Year 2060," writing from the viewpoint of an eighty-seven-year-old.

As the project got underway, students were eager to share their letters aloud—the ones they wrote as well as the ones they received. They took special pains to edit and revise, and wrote their final drafts on school stationery. (I drew lines on one sheet of stationery and had it photocopied in various colors.)

At the end of the semester we planned a pen-pal get-together, and students met their pen pals for the first time.

Once the seniors came to the middle school, and students entertained them by reading their best writings. Another time students were invited to a "Make Your Own Ice-Cream-Sundae Party" at the nursing home, during which they and their pen pals buried a time capsule of writings.

The pen-pal program was a great success. Several students have requested that they be allowed back into the program next year. And one husky football player mumbled to me last month, "You know, I like this class better than gym now."

Iris Epstein, Hendrick Hudson School District, Montrose, New York

CELEBRITIES CELEBRATE READING

As part of a recent celebration of reading, I had students write to celebrities and ask them to name their favorite book and explain what impact it made on them. Celebrities were also asked for a photograph; the letters, responses, and photographs were shared with the entire student body in a public display. After I presented this idea to my students, I followed the basic steps described here:

1. Students and I brainstormed for celebrities to write to. On the chalkboard I listed such possible categories as authors, actors, musicians, comedians, political leaders, religious leaders, businessmen, sports figures, pro wrestlers, models, and royalty. I passed around twenty-six sheets of paper, each headed by a letter of the alphabet. Students added to the sheets as many names as they could think of, and at the end of the class period I collected the sheets and entered the names on our computer data base. (Between two of my classes, students came up with five hundred names.)

2. My students chose to write a class form letter, and agreed that the final letter should:

    explain that the purpose of the project is to raise student consciousness regarding the importance of reading;
    ask for an 8" x 10" glossy photograph;
    ask for a brief statement about the celebrity's favorite book and the impact it made;
    for a return address, use the school address, in care of the teacher.

    All students wrote drafts of the letter, and a committee made up of students prepared a final version of the class letter from the drafts. Then, with the form letter on disk, students were able to make copies of the letter and print out individualized versions, adding personal comments if they wished to.

3. Hoping to receive fifty or so replies, we planned to send several hundred letters. This required that students in two classes send at least four letters each. To divide the list of celebrities fairly

7

among all the students, I cut the complete, alphabetized list of celebrities' names in strips, each strip containing about eight names. I put the strips in a hat and let students draw. From one strip of eight names, each student was to choose at least four celebrities to send letters to, obtaining their addresses from books of addresses in the library. Any students who were disappointed at not drawing the name of their favorite celebrities were encouraged to write to these celebrities on their own for a personal reply.

After five or six weeks, enough replies had come in for us to arrange an impressive display in a display case in the main hall of our school. When possible, we also displayed copies of the books that were mentioned in the letters.

Linda Meixner, Parma High School, Ohio

If You Can Convince Mom and Dad,
YOU CAN CONVINCE ANYONE

I have had great success with this persuasive writing assignment. Parents seem to enjoy it as much as students, and it's a topic sure to be mentioned during parent-teacher conferences. First I give the students the following directions:

The *purpose* of this assignment is to persuade your parents (you may work with one parent if you prefer) to allow you to do something they do not want you to do. Or, you may adopt the opposite scenario: your parents are insisting that you do something you do not want to do. The *form* of the assignment will be a two-page (minimum) letter to your parents in which you attempt to win their permission. You may use the personal letter form or a business format.

The *audience,* of course, will be your parents—an audience opposed to what you have to say. Finally, follow this *procedure*:

1. Get a list of opposing arguments from your parents. The more arguments they provide, the easier your task will probably be. I'll help you out by writing an explanatory letter for you to take home.
2. Review the aspects of persuasive writing we have discussed in class before you begin your letter: the use of rhetorical questions, antithesis, tone, logic, anticipation of and response to your opponent's arguments.
3. Turn in your parents' list with the final copy of your letter. Your letter will not be graded, however, until you have shared it with your parents and obtained a parental signature.

After I have defined the assignment for students, I ask them to give the following letter to their parents. I allow several days for students to obtain their lists before they begin their persuasive replies.

Dear Parents:

I am working with students on persuasive writing. A major problem in this kind of writing is anticipating the arguments of the opposition and responding satisfactorily to those arguments.

I would like your assistance for one writing assignment. Since almost all teenagers would very much like to do at least one thing that their parents have forbidden, I have chosen that parent-teen scenario for this persuasive writing assignment. Your son or daughter is to choose the specific topic. As preparation, he or she will ask you to list all of your reasons for opposition. I've suggested below how such a scenario might go.

Student topic: I want to redecorate my room.
Parental objections:

1. It's too expensive.
2. You never even clean your room; why decorate?
3. You already spend too much time there. We only see you at meals as it is now.
4. You never spend any time in your room; why should we bother?
5. Your brother (sister) is going to feel left out. We can't start redecorating everyone's room.

6. Your taste in interior decoration is questionable. We can't paint ceilings and walls in school colors or indulge in other such fads.
7. I'll end up doing all the work. I don't have the time or the energy.
8. It'll cost too much.
9. I said "No!"

Some of your objections may be difficult to refute, but don't hold back. I want students to be challenged by realistic opposition.

After students have brought in your arguments, they will write letters to you answering those objections. I am requiring your son or daughter to show you this final letter. It's only fair that you should consider the counter arguments! Your signature on that letter indicating that you have read it will be satisfactory. A written response to your son or daughter or to me would be delightful.

Thank you for your support.

Sincerely,

M. Trudy Adams

M. Trudy Adams, Ypsilanti High School, Ypsilanti, Michigan

WRITING ACROSS BOUNDARIES

You're probably familiar with the idea of exchanging composition papers between classes. However, the most success I've had with this endeavor actually involved exchanging papers with a class in another state. In each of the past several years, I have exchanged four sets of ninth-grade composition papers with the teacher of a junior high class from the neighboring state of Idaho. You should be able to find your own exchange partner by contacting an English department chairperson in a nearby state.

Not only are students especially interested in their student neighbors, but this project seems to provide an increased sense of audience and a feeling of pride in writing. I use the following format:

Step 1: At the beginning of the school year, teachers agree on four specified times throughout the school year (once per nine weeks in my case) at which they will exchange student papers on set topics. The topics we agreed on for the past year were:

a. Describe your school and its surroundings.
b. Describe a typical school day.
c. Tell as much about yourself and your family as you like.
d. Describe the community in which you live. (For example, what do people do for a living? for entertainment? etc.)

Step 2: Once the topics and dates have been chosen, my colleague in Idaho and I assign the first writing topic, giving students a full week in class. We don't allow students to work on the assignment at home unless they are sick or absent, and then we stipulate that they spend no more than the allotted time. This encourages students to use their class time responsibly and ensures that the papers exchanged by the two classes reflect a similar investment of time and effort. It also allows the teacher to see students' daily progress and pinpoint areas of difficulty.

Step 3: On the last of the five days, all papers are mailed by both teachers. When the papers arrive from the exchange class, a separate comment sheet is attached and students are encouraged to write brief comments and opinions on what they read. To prevent the comment sheets from becoming too negative in tone, encourage students to write three positive comments for every criticism. In addition, just in case you have a student or two who can't resist the inappropriate phrase or epithet, you might want to read over the comment sheets before they are returned. After a day or two for reading and comment writing, mail papers back to the originating teacher. The papers and comment sheets you receive back will give your students at least a full class period of reading and discussion about their student neighbors across the state line.

Ed Sansom, Cut Bank High School, Cut Bank, Montana

WRITING TO WHOM IT MAY CONCERN

No matter how much emphasis is placed on the importance of audience in a writing assignment, most high school students remain unimpressed. After all, even the most gullible freshman knows perfectly well that the real audience is the teacher. In order to move my sophomores away from such a misconception, I make the following assignment on audience as a part of their introduction to the writing process.

First I decide how many groups to divide the class into—usually six or seven groups of four—and make up an equal number of topics with four possible audiences each. Three sample topics are given below.

1. Write a paragraph discussing your reactions to high school life.
    Audience 1   Parents
    Audience 2   Best friend
    Audience 3   Someone you have a crush on
    Audience 4   Favorite teacher
2. Write a paragraph explaining why you were out after midnight.
    Audience 1   Parents
    Audience 2   Best friend
    Audience 3   Arresting officer
    Audience 4   Younger sibling
3. Write a paragraph explaining a page of test answers found under your desk after a test.
    Audience 1   Classmates at the lunch table
    Audience 2   English teacher
    Audience 3   Parents
    Audience 4   Guidance counselor

Once groups are formed, each member is given a slip of paper listing the group topic and his or her particular audience. Students are instructed to write a paragraph on the topic to the person(s) listed on the slip. No group discussion is permitted.

When the writing is completed—I find timed writing works well—I ask students to talk in their groups about their results, again with a time limit. We spend the remainder of the period in discussion of the purpose of the assignment and its effectiveness.

Although I don't evaluate the paragraphs, I do collect them and display them in group packets to be read by other class members. I especially like this assignment because student response is good and it clearly illustrates the influence of audience in writing. In addition, it is one of the few group assignments I make with the full confidence that everyone will pull his or her own weight.

Mary Parker, Incarnate Word Academy, St. Louis, Missouri

MADISON AVENUE
and the Composition Classroom

Helping students understand the concept of *audience* is not always an easy job for the composition teacher. Many students view composition assignments as graded exercises that don't extend beyond the classroom, so the idea of identifying someone who would want to read their writing seems somewhat strange to them. I've begun to look not just for verbal explanations of audience but for visual explanations as well.

Magazine advertisements can be an effective classroom tool at both the high school and college levels, especially since there are many magazines aimed at the interests of the young consumer, such as *Seventeen*, *Car and Driver*, and the music magazine *Spin*. Other useful magazines are *Sports Illustrated*, *Field and Stream*, *Working Woman*, and *Parents*, all of which are aimed at audiences with specialized values and interests.

Usually, I begin the discussion by placing the students in small groups of three or four, giving each group two ads aimed at completely different audiences (women/men or parents/single adults). I don't tell the students the sources of the ads; I ask them instead to determine for themselves not just an ad's audience but also the way in which the ad appeals to an audience either in its verbal or visual message. Features I ask them to consider include (1) the role a person may play within an ad, such as businessperson or homemaker, (2) the gender and age of the characters, and (3) the values being stressed, for example, responsibility, leisure, prestige, or romance.

After groups have formed their opinions, I reveal the source of each ad, which in most cases makes the intended audience clear. Students then compare the actual audience with the audience they had inferred. Students often prove very adept at identifying an ad's audience.

In addition, I ask the students to bring in one advertisement from any magazine they read on a regular basis to share with the other members of their groups. I ask students to consider (1) the reasons they chose the ad; (2) whether the product advertised is something they really want or need; and (3) whether the ad would actually influence them to buy the product. On the basis of group feedback for each of the ads, the students write a critique of their respective ads, analyzing what messages the ad uses to appeal to them as an audience and also how effective such messages are.

Through the resulting discussion, students are able to recognize the importance of audience, not only in advertising but in their own discourses as well. I usually give this assignment early in the semester, and I have found that it helps students determine the audience in subsequent assignments and makes them aware of the need for a writer to take audience into consideration when making content and style choices.

Kristine Blair, Purdue University, West Lafayette, Indiana

| TWO-FACED WRITING

Adults in our society come into contact with a wide variety of written materials every day, from political pamphlets to bargain fliers. I use a special writing assignment to help students become more discriminating readers. Students write two paragraphs based on the same facts, with a different purpose in mind for each paragraph. By writing to achieve two different purposes, students develop a sense for how fact selection and purpose alter the effect of a message. This lesson can be carried over to the evaluation of any written material they encounter.

I ask students to write two separate paragraphs as described below. They must draw all their facts from the fact list, but some facts may be omitted if desired.

Paragraph 1
Audience: Tourists contemplating a Caribbean vacation
Tone: Positive, highly enthusiastic
Assignment: Write an advertising brochure for the San Ladida Chamber of Commerce. Your purpose is to convince tourists that San Ladida is the best place to choose for a winter vacation. Remember, your livelihood depends on tourists!

Paragraph 2
Audience: Newspaper readers, especially anyone contemplating a Caribbean vacation
Tone: Highly negative, almost hostile
Assignment: Write an editorial for the *Miami Herald.* You are aware of San Ladida's attempt to build its tourist trade, but you feel that the island's environmental, political, and social problems make it unsuitable, even potentially dangerous, for visitors. You see yourself as a concerned citizen who believes in consumer protection.

Fact List
1. *Description*
   located in the Caribbean Sea south of St. Thomas
   thirty miles long and ten to twenty miles wide
   features a four-mile stretch of white sand beach suitable for swimming
   jellyfish relatively common
   last shark sighting in September 1983
   most parts of island covered by dense brush, populated portions of island connected by thin trails and winding roads
   Mt. Vivacious, an active volcano, last erupted in October 1983
   rainy season December through March; sunny, warm weather the remainder of the year
   governed by General R.D. Thomas
2. *Recreation*
   boat excursions on *The Shark*
   snorkeling
   bicycling and hiking, guide recommended
   hotel gambling casinos
3. *Economic/social situation*
   high inflation

crime rate up 20% since 1983

hostility flares occasionally between low-income, year-round residents of the north and west shore and members of the resort community on the south shore

To emphasize the contrast between the words and tone used in each paragraph, students can present the final writings to the class in pairs. One student reads the editorial aloud, and the other student follows by reading the advertising brochure version. This presentation sparks discussion of how the two paragraphs differ in tone and how words can be selected to create certain nuances.

J. Neighbors, Simsbury High School, Simsbury, Connecticut

| WHAT A CHARACTER!

When students choose friends, they rely on a sense of what personality traits they like and dislike. They can use that same analytical ability to evaluate characters in stories.

I ask students to write a letter to their parents telling them about a fellow student that they want to bring home for the weekend. This assignment works well with college students who live away from home, but it can also work with high school students, who can be asked to imagine that they are inviting friends to visit their families. The students know that their families may like some things about the guest and dislike other things. The purpose of the letter is to prepare the parents for the potential guest. The twist is that the guest is a fictional character chosen by the student.

In composing their letters, the students will have to analyze the quirks of both the character and their parents. Will the family be fooled by the first impression? Will the character get along with the family? What discussion topics should be avoided? How should the family act around the guest? Students can also consider the conflict that the character encountered in the story. Can the family perhaps help with the conflict? Or should mention of the conflict be avoided?

Before students begin writing, I emphasize the importance of some basic criteria for analyzing and describing characters:

1.   Physical appearance and background (clothes, posture, makeup, hairstyle; cultural, ethnic, racial, and religious origins)
2.   What they say, how they say it, and what others say about them (thoughts, hopes, beliefs, fears, feelings, motivations)
3.   How they act and react towards self or others (actions may "speak louder than words")

As students have fun with this assignment, they gain insights into the characters, their own families, and themselves. They may also begin to consider relationships between people in new ways as they think about personality makeup and how particular traits influence how people act.

Marilen Wegner, Eastern Illinois University, Charleston, Illinois

WRITINGS FROM THE NURSERY

My students often have difficulty in understanding the importance of audience for successfully communicating a message and influencing word choice and writing style. I devised the following exercise to help students understand inductively the importance of audience. To give students a familiar situation, I chose to use nursery rhymes. These are well known and lend themselves to clever writing assignments in audience, as well as in purpose and point of view.

I begin the lesson by sharing "Mary Had a Little Lamb" with the class. I do not explain at this point what the goal of the lesson is, preferring that students reach the conclusion themselves later on. Separate small groups are assigned one each of the following topics for five minutes of freewriting:

1. Mary's journal entry for that day
2. Mary's letter to a friend
3. the teacher's discipline report to the principal
4. the principal's letter to Mary's parents explaining her suspension from school
5. Mary's parents' protest to the school board requesting that Mary's suspension be revoked
6. a feature story in the local paper

Following the freewriting, a student from each group is asked to read his or her paper. Next, I ask, "What differences do you notice in the pieces of writing?" Students quickly notice a difference in word choice and style of writing. Then I ask, "What do you think accounts for those differences in word choice and style?" One student may point out that Mary was writing to herself in her journal but to a friend in the letter. Comparing the principal's letter and the parents' protest, the students perceive that purpose as well as audience determines the style of writing. The newspaper story with an objective point of view and larger audience further changes the style.

There are numerous other nursery rhymes that are suitable. These are just a few that I have used with success with all grade levels:

"Three Little Kittens"
1. a lost ad
2. a found ad
3. Dr. Spock's advice to parents on handling children who lose things
4. instructions to kittens on how to prevent losing their clothing

"Jack and Jill"
1. a front-page news story
2. the paramedics' accident report
3. Jack and Jill's excuse to their parents on why they did not return with the water
4. the parents' letter to the town council requesting movement of the well or the clearing of a safer path to the well

"Old King Cole"
1. a society editor's story of a social evening at Old King Cole's palace
2. a fiddler's letter home telling about his new job and his new boss, Old King Cole
3. the Queen's memo to the King complaining about the time he is

spending with "the fiddlers three"

4. a music critic's review of "the fiddlers three"
5. King Cole's official royal biographer's journal

Through experimenting with different writing styles and talking about audience, students become aware of how and why they might vary the style and word choice in personal writings outside of class.

Diane Chandler, Barboursville High School, Barboursville, West Virginia

NEED AN AUDIENCE? WRITE A LETTER

"There's a singular and perpetual charm in a letter. . ."
—Thomas Bailey Aldrich (American writer, 1836-1907)

As a writing assignment, the letter serves many practical purposes for the student. It provides practice in writing concisely and communicating for a purpose and can help build confidence in students who feel daunted by longer, more formal writing assignments. In addition, a letter-writing assignment can allow the teacher to evaluate students' knowledge and empathy toward an author or character in a literary work.

For the Romantics, Edgar Allan Poe offers a worthwhile opportunity for letter writing. The narrator of either "The Raven" or "The Fall of the House of Usher" could write to Sigmund Freud for advice. The letter could explain the narrator's current state of mind and the events that led to this state of depression or fear. Such a letter would allow students to present the plot of the poem or story, recounting as many details as needed to allow Dr. Freud to provide a remedy.

One of my favorite letter-writing assignments from the twentieth century follows the American Short Story series film adapted from F. Scott Fitzgerald's "Bernice Bobs Her Hair." In the story, Bernice, visiting her "cool" cousin Marjorie, conforms to the crowd by flirting with boys so she can be popular. Her new image causes her to boast that she will bob her hair, a boast that was helped along by Marjorie, who is now jealous of her popularity. Not wanting to back down, Bernice makes good her boast, with disastrous results. Now she must return to Eau Claire and her mother. Ask students to write a letter from Bernice to her mother explaining what she did, but more important, why she did it. It gives students real insight into peer pressure and the desire to be "in."

Finally, if you and your students would like to see a particular author on a commemorative stamp, consider this as an opportunity for more letter writing, this time to the members of the advisory board. (Try addressing your letters in care of the Postmaster General, Postal Service Philatelic Unit, Washington, DC 20265, or contact your local post office for information.) We wrote letters in the spring of 1988 in support of a Hemingway stamp, and in July of 1989 the stamp was issued. Maybe we helped, maybe not. The students thought they did, so what else matters?

Craig Akey, Clintonville High School, Clintonville, Wisconsin

THE WRITING PROCESS IN ACTION

Writers must make many choices as they commit words to paper. They need to appreciate the ranges of choice available to them in content, in rhetorical stance, in organizational pattern, and in linguistic structure. They need to understand how their choices will enhance or degrade the quality of the written piece and how their choices will affect the responses of their readers. The primary means of learning how to make the best decisions seems to be complex, continuing writing experiences closely examined by sensitive respondents.

MAKING CHOICES OF RHETORICAL STANCE

Writers usually make assumptions about rhetorical stance when they write, whether they realize it or not. The typical school writer assumes the *voice* of the uncertain student, addresses the *audience* of teacher as critic and grade-giver, has the *purpose* of getting an A or B, and uses whatever *form* the teacher has proposed. Rhetorical stance becomes a valid arena for choice when the writer carefully and judiciously considers a *range* of possibilities in voice, audience, purpose, and form, and then makes decisions appropriate to the specific writing task at hand.

Voice

One might guess that the writer is a writer—and that's that. But each of us is called upon to fill many real roles, and we can project ourselves imaginatively into many others. That whole range of roles awaits the student writer in choosing a voice. Is he or she writing as a tenth grader in Ms. E's class? (Class clown? Class dolt? Class whiz?) As brother or sister to an adoring younger sibling? As dutiful child? As new boyfriend or girlfriend? As star tennis player? As true friend? As sworn enemy? As the writer clearly establishes his or her own specific voice for any particular paper, he or she then can make the appropriate choices of content and language, of emphasis and tone.

Instructional methods to sensitize students to voice, to help them develop a sense of voice in their writing, follow:

1. Select a school issue on which there is divided opinion (progress reports, smoking areas, detention). Have students try two paragraphs on the same subject, one as the angry critic and one as the satisfied supporter. Then have students analyze the differences in word choice, metaphoric language, sentence length, etc.
2. Having selected some subject of adolescent concern (staying out too late, getting bad grades, getting a traffic ticket, cutting class), have students prepare internal dialogues between their fearful, self-critical voices and their reassuring, self-confident voices.
3. Having completed the reading of a literary piece, have the students write conversations between themselves and characters in the story about the events in the plot. They may assume a critical voice (e.g., with Walter Mitty) or a sympathetic voice (e.g., with Juliet).

Audience

Sensitivity to audience can make important differences in the way a written piece turns out. In considering their audiences, writers need to consider:

Who is the reader?
How sophisticated on this subject is the reader?
How ready is the reader to receive this "message"?
What help does the reader need?
What preformed opinions will this reader have?

The audience for any writing activity can be designated as part of the assignment or it can exist naturally in the writing situation; it can be simulated or real. Particular attention needs to be paid to *how* writers tune their messages to their audiences. Writers might articulate the audience clues in their pieces for their classmates as a way to illuminate audiences as a variable.

Activities to develop a sense of audience include the following:

1. Select a well-known local event (sports event, accident, school activity, celebration). Have students write two versions, one for a person who knows the general scene but missed this particular event (e.g., an absent classmate) and one for a person not at all familiar with either the setting or the event (e.g., a faraway relative). Contrast the two versions in class discussion.

2. Ask the students to assume they've received what they feel is a totally unfair second-semester grade in English. First, they are to write to Mr. Z, who is known to be intolerant of student opinions, very sure of himself, and very hard to talk to. The writer did not get along well in class with Mr. Z. Then have them assume Ms. Y was the teacher. Ms. Y has the reputation of being very fair and reasonable. She had been fun in class, and the writer had gotten on well with her. Students should compare the two versions, noting the audience clues.

3. Writers are to take a subject they know well (osmosis, internal combustion engines, classical music, making brownies) and explain some part of it very clearly in writing to an eight year old. Students should be cautioned about the use of overly technical terms.

Purpose

There are many possible purposes to writing—to inform, to soothe, to persuade, to upset, to confirm, to explain, to record, and to entertain, among others. The purpose selected becomes another controlling factor in the way a writing piece will be developed. An informational piece would more likely select important facts and present them in a straightforward way, while a persuasive one might, deliberately or not, omit or distort some facts while embellishing others. Writers must experiment with purpose and the way it affects writing so they may make responsible choices of purpose and make those choices work in the writing stage.

Instructional activities which will give the writer experience with the variable of purpose include the following:

1. Select a local problem which is well know to the students (school, community, environmental, political). After discussing the issue thoroughly in class, ask students to write to two different purposes: one to *persuade* a responsible public official to take a particular course of action and the other to *entertain* a same-age friend who is away in a foreign land as an exchange student. Follow up with a small-group comparison-contrast analysis as a way to get at how different purposes changed the pieces.

2. Distribute copies of single-product advertisements. Ask the students to rewrite the information given there into an information piece for a consumer column in the local newspaper. Examine sample papers in a class discussion to see how a change in purpose changed the presentation.

Form

Decisions about voice, audience, and purpose, coupled with a clear sense of content, usually lead very plainly to a particular form. A concerned citizen wishing to persuade her congressperson about a course of action on acid rain quite properly selects a business letter form. A young swain wishing to restate his strong feelings for his high school sweetheart would be more likely to choose a poetry form than a display ad. At any rate, a choice of form is necessary at the beginning of the writing stage.

Forms abound in our complicated culture; instruction in writing should include some passing experience with many of them and in-depth experience with some, experience enough to make them familiar to students and to make students comfortable with them. Sample activities for such purposes include the following:

1. Distribute copies of pieces done in a variety of public forms (possibilities include editorials, news articles, legal documents, myths, essays, how-to-do-it articles, magazine fiction, advice columns, children's stories, tall tales, and want ads). Ask each student to do a brief oral report on the piece he or she has received, commenting particularly on the form, how it works, and how it is appropriate to audience and purpose.

2. Distribute copies of letters to the editor. Have students try converting them into some other form used in a newspaper. After reading some aloud, discuss how well the alternate form works.

A list of some of our culture's writing forms follows.

Some Discourse Forms for Content Writing

Journals and diaries
  (real or imaginary)
Biographical sketches
Anecdotes and stories:
  from experience
  as told by others
Thumbnail sketches:
  of famous people
  of places
  of content ideas
  of historical events
Guess who/what descriptions
Letters:
  personal reactions
  observations
  public/informational
  persuasive:
  to the editor
  to public officials
  to imaginary people
  from imaginary places
Requests
Applications
Memos
Résumés and summaries
Poems
Plays
Stories, such as:
  fantasy
  adventure
  science fiction
  historical
Dialogues and conversations
Children's books
Telegrams
Editorials
Commentaries
Responses and rebuttals
Newspaper "fillers"
Fact books or fact sheets
School newspaper stories
Stories or essays for local papers
Case studies:
  school problems
  local issues
  national concerns
  historical problems

Reviews:
  books (including textbooks)
  fiction or nonfiction films
  fiction or nonfiction television programs
  music
Historical "you are there" scenes
Science notes:
  observations
  science notebooks
  reading reports
  lab reports
Math:
  story problems
  solutions to problems
  record books
  notes and observations
Responses to literature
Proposals:
  utopian
  practical
Interviews:
  actual
  imaginary
Directions:
  how-to
  school or neighborhood guide
  survival manual
Dictionaries and lexicons
Technical reports
Future options, notes on:
  careers, employments
  school and training
  military/public service
Written debates
Essays taking a stand on:
  school issues
  family problems
  state or national issues
  moral questions
  Books and booklets
Informational monographs
Scripts:
  radio
  TV
  dramatic
  film or slide-show
  Notes for improvised drama

scientific issues	Cartoons and cartoon strips
Songs and ballads	Puzzles and word searches
Demonstrations	Prophecy and predictions
Poster displays	Photographs and captions
	Collages, montages, mobiles, and
	sculptures incorporating
	written language

Reprinted from Chapter Two in The Writing Process in Action *(NCTE, 1986) by Jackie Proett and Kent Gill.*

APPROPRIATING THE QUERY

As a seasoned English teacher and freelance writer, I know the importance of planning before I begin to write. To help students acquire the planning habit, I borrowed the query from professional writers. The query, a letter from a writer to an editor, seeks approval to write an article on a particular subject, but its importance in my writing program is that it forces young authors to formulate their ideas before tackling a writing assignment.

Following a discussion of the assignment, each student writes a letter to me, known in this case as the editor, in which he or she explains the topic, the audience for whom the writing is intended, and a proposed method of development. If I approve the query, the student proceeds with an outline and first draft. Those who submit unacceptable queries revise them until they can clearly express to me what and why they are writing.

The query encourages students to think through their ideas, to identify their audiences, and to justify writing about given topics. The query also gives students an opportunity to test an idea before advancing to the next stage of the writing process.

Suzanna Colby, Chaparral High School, Scottsdale, Arizona

SELLING ROCK 'N' ROLL TO THE PTA

This whimsical activity brings home to students the necessity of clarifying audience and purpose in a piece of writing and brings to life the normally straightforward task of letter writing.

Before class, prepare and photocopy two lists of about twenty-five items each: one a list of objects or products, and the other a list of groups of people. Some possible items are listed below:

Objects

1. purple and green striped denim bib overalls
2. ankle-high Nike running shoes
3. peppermint patties
4. complete set of *History of Rock and Roll in America* in twenty records
5. carrot curlers
6. asbestos gloves
7. eyeglass frames (no lenses)
8. 2" plastic statuettes of William Shakespeare

Audiences

1. Speed Kings Motorcycle Group of Loma Linda, California
2. members of Parent Teachers Association of Pleasant Ridge, Wisconsin
3. English faculty of Wakhetenee High School, Wakhetenee, Idaho
4. parolees from the Ohio minimum security prison system
5. members of Early Morning Bird Watchers of Greater Utah
6. Young Liberals for Freedom political group of upstate New York
7. Chamber of Commerce of Riptide, Michigan
8. Petal Pushers Garden Club of Blossom City, Indiana

Next, arrange students in groups of four to six members. Each group is to consider itself a "company" that has excess items to sell. Ask each company to pick two numbers from 1 to 25 (to correspond to your lists of objects and audiences); cross off the numbers as they are chosen so that no two companies have the same numbers. Then distribute copies of your lists and describe the assignment. The first number picked by students determines what *object* their company must sell, and the second number determines the *audience* to whom they must sell their items. For example, a company might end up selling carrot curlers (#5) to the Young Liberals for Freedom (#6), or Nikes to the PTA. Members of the company must discuss the selling qualities of the item and the uses that the item would have for the target group, and, finally, they must compose a letter designed to persuade the target group to buy the item. Students may also, if they wish, prepare an ad, an appropriate slogan, or a brochure of features.

Be sure to think of a way for the groups to "show off" their efforts—whether by posting the letters on the bulletin board or by having a member of each company read the group's letter aloud. But be forewarned: this exercise produces rather riotous results.

Gratia Murphy, Youngstown State University, Youngstown, Ohio

| DEAR ARTIST

Picture yourself dressed in your favorite clothes and posed in front of the fireplace with your right hand casually touching the richly carved mantel. On the mantel is the trophy you won in a figure skating competition. Is this the way you would want to be remembered? Are these the prized possessions you would select to have included in a portrait of you? How and where would you want to be posed? With what or whom would you want to be pictured?

I ask my students to write a letter to a famous portrait artist in an attempt to commission that painter or photographer to create the perfect remembrance of the student. There must be a paragraph in which the student develops the reason(s) for wanting the portrait. Also required are the answers to the questions posed above and the reasons for each response. Why should each person or item be included? Of what significance is the setting? The writers may include other information or arguments for what they feel is necessary.

Prewriting activities include discussions mentioning artists, the viewing of prints of portraits, a review of possible sources if research is needed, and the sharing of anecdotes about prized possessions. H. W. Janson's *History of Art for Young People* (Harry N. Abrams, 1971) is available in my classroom as an aid to students during all phases of writing. When the discussion of the assignment is initiated, the class and I discuss the following portraits which are found in Janson's book:

Raphael. *Pope Leo with His Nephews Cardinal Giulio de'Medici and Luigi de'Rossi.* (colorplate 34, page 191).
Hans Holbein the Younger. *Henry VIII.* (colorplate 43, page 228).
Anthony van Dyck. *James Stuart, Duke of Lennox.* (figure 237, page 242).
Thomas Gainsborough. *Robert Andrews and His Wife.* (colorplate 55, page 268).
Francisco Goya. *The Family of Charles IV.* (figure 272, page 283).
James A. McNeill Whistler. *Arrangement in Black and Gray: The Artist's Mother.* (figure 301, page 311).

The required format is a business letter. This always leads some students to go to impressive lengths researching actual addresses for artists long deceased. (How would you go about finding Michelangelo's "mailing address"?) Many students, however, will simply want to invent addresses.

Students may choose to take any tone or point of view in their effort to be persuasive. A few of my students' letters have been especially memorable for their exaggeration—either in their flattery of the artist about earlier works or in the generosity with which they open financial negotiations.

In their finished form, with details and explanations of significant people and possessions, the persuasive letters are themselves intriguing self-portraits of the student writers.

Margaret H. Clark, Valley View Middle School, Watchung, New Jersey

| WRITING FOR READERS

The problem with many of the writing assignments I see used in high school and college composition classes is that they encourage students to view writing as an activity which occurs in a vacuum, with no effect or importance outside the classroom walls. For this reason, I agree with Britton, Graves, and others that having students write and send letters to real audiences is a valid and important activity in any writing class. The following assignment is one that has worked well for me and my students in the past, and I hope that it (or some variation of it) can be helpful to other composition teachers as well. The assignment has two parts.

In Part I, I ask my students to state a problem with an institution of some sort—a place of employment, a social or political organization, or even the school itself. I have them direct their invention and prewriting energies in two different directions: (1) define the current problem completely, and (2) speculate about what the causes of that problem might be.

Next, the students decide on three audiences to whom they would like to write letters about this problem. There are, however, restrictions and guidelines for arriving at three adequate audiences: (1) one audience must be extremely informal (friend, parent, etc.) and one extremely formal (someone in a position of power within the institution, perhaps); (2) one audience must be an extreme insider to the problem, must know as much as, or more than, the writer knows about the problem, and one must be an extreme outsider, must know nearly nothing about the problem at hand; and (3) at least one of the audiences must be able to do something to help solve the problem.

Once the problem has been adequately defined and the audiences meet all the criteria for the assignment, I usually encourage my students to role-play for a while; they freewrite about the problem as if they were the audience members to whom they will soon write. The amount of freewriting will depend, of course, on how much of an insider or outsider the audience in question is: an outsider who knows little about the problem at hand will have little to say about it, but an insider will have much to say. I often ask students to divide their freewriting from the insider perspective into two parts: "knowledge" (or what the audience already knows about the problem) and "attitude" (or how the audience feels about the problem).

Then, using the information they have discovered in all of their freewriting, the students start to write the letters. The students will begin to notice that the nature of their language and the amount of content they use in their letters will change according to the insider/outsider and formal/informal nature of their audiences. I encourage the students to pursue these differences in language and content and to write and revise according to the needs and expectations of their individual audiences.

With all three letters finished, many students see something they have never perceived before: how writing changes according to audience. But this is not enough. The most effective assignments not only ask students to execute a task, but they also ask students to articulate reasons for the choices they made in its execution. Thus, in Part II of this assignment, I ask the students to analyze the changes they made in language and content across all three letters.

I ask the students to write one paragraph on the language in each letter, using quotations from their letters to support their arguments, and one paragraph on the content in each letter, indicating parts of the letters which illustrate their claims.

The assignment, then, as a whole, must be turned in. I ask for photocopies and the originals of the three letters, and SASEs. I grade the photocopied letters and mail the originals to their intended audiences. Not surprisingly, more than half of the students receive replies to their letters almost immediately. During the next assignment, as more students receive replies, we begin each class period by reading some of them and discussing the impact these letters had on those particular audiences.

Sadly enough, it is through this assignment that many of my students realize for the first time that their writing is actually taken seriously outside the walls of the composition classroom. This realization appears to have a good effect on their motivation and interest in my class, and I only hope that it helps them in their lives as well as their future academic careers.

Bruce McComiskey, Purdue University, West Lafayette, Indiana

2 | EMPHASIS: PREWRITING AND DRAFTING

PREWRITING AS MOTIVATION

Many students bring to writing a negative attitude; some even bring a fear of writing. Extended opportunities for prewriting reduce that hostility and help take away that fear. Prewriting puts excitement back into language study and helps students understand the writing process. While students will continue to believe that writing is hard work—and it is—they will also begin to see that writing is challenging and fun.

Prewriting, of course, is an integral part of the writing process, a step that takes place before each piece of writing is to be done. In addition, I suggest scheduling a series of prewriting activities prior to the introduction of the writing unit or program. Both situations are discussed below.

PREWRITING PRIOR TO A WRITING UNIT

Prewriting activities that precede a writing unit should encourage students to experiment with words and phrases without penalty, to find out what works for them and what doesn't. Students can also investigate the effective uses of language by other writers. They can work with abstractions, consider clichés, discuss word derivations and coinages, experiment with metaphor.

Talking is also an important part of prewriting. Inexperienced writers think they have nothing to say, so students should spend time discussing ideas that interest them—school activities, sports, cafeteria meals, hobbies, community problems.

The following prewriting activities help students become interested in language and develop a positive attitude toward writing. Although all may be used as individual assignments, take advantage of the inherently verbal nature of groups. Adapt some activities for small groups and use others as the basis for all-class brainstorming sessions.

1. Each student jots down a half-dozen words that describe a pet. Encourage students to try for unique words, ones that discriminate. Most cats are independent: but Tiger is a loner, Lady Jade exclusive, and Sam a bum. Some mutts are cocky, others are servile. Students

then clip pictures from newspapers and magazines that represent their descriptive words. Later, they read their word lists aloud as classmates try to guess the pet being described. Finally, the pictures are shared, and the discussion focuses on why a given picture suggests the meaning of a given word.

2. Students search through the sports pages and record the many different expressions used to communicate that one team has won or lost to another: *walloped, rolled over, swamped, demolished, scrambled.* Encourage students to add expressions of their own. This leads to a discussion of the power of verbs.

3. Students collect and talk about examples of lively language: bumper stickers, billboards, license plates, graffiti, T-shirts, media messages, book titles (real or imagined), popular lyrics, slang.

4. Students create visual representations of common expressions:

down in the dumps	DdUoMwPnS
mixed-up kid	IDK
man in the moon	MOmanON

5. Ask students to list words that appeal to each of the five senses; words like *glare, velvety, fishy, screech.* Discuss what happens when we use a word commonly associated with one sense in another context: loud colors (screaming red?), a sour note on the trumpet, tough talk, a harsh or smooth taste. Then have students jot down five favorite foods and list under each any descriptive words that appeal to the sense of taste. Using the same foods, ask them to come up with a sight, sound, smell, and touch word for each food. Spaghetti is bland, but it's also pale, silent, moist, and slippery.

PREWRITING BEFORE SPECIFIC ASSIGNMENTS

Prewriting that immediately precedes the act of writing is consistent with the kinds of readiness found in other performance areas: consider the warm-up exercises practiced by athletes, musicians, singers, and actors. Students also need time to get ready to write. Perhaps they may jot down notes about ideas to include, or they may recognize that they need to learn more about a topic in order to write about it.

The following activities suggest the kinds of prewriting that immediately precede the writing activity and provide the motivation for it.

Topic: Pets
Prewriting activity. Discuss together the human qualities of any well-known animal in the comics—Snoopy, for example. List these qualities on the chalkboard. How do they fit the general category—dog? How do they create

a unique dog—Snoopy? What is the effect of assigning human qualities to an animal?

Writing assignment. Students develop a piece of writing (story, description, series of comic strips) in which a real or imagined pet takes on these or other human qualities.

Topic: Dialogue

Prewriting activity. Collect in advance pictures that show two or more people speaking to one another. Settings may vary from automobiles to street corners to an elegant hotel dining room. Do not distribute the pictures until the writing begins. Introduce the activity by talking about the importance of dialogue in establishing character and developing plot. Consider examples from the class anthology or other sources. You may want to review the punctuation of dialogue. Then introduce a topic of current interest to students.

Writing assignment. Distribute the pictures and ask students to involve the people in their pictures in a dialogue about the topic introduced during the prewriting activity.

Topic: Childhood Memories

Prewriting activity. Students bring childhood pictures to class. Others besides the students may be included in the pictures, and snapshots are as useful as studio photographs. Share these pictures, talking about setting, occasion, and other special attributes.

Writing assignment. Each student relates in writing an incident suggested by the childhood picture he or she brought to class (a personal recollection, a story, a piece focusing on alternate points of view—that of the mother, the child, the photographer, for instance).

Topic: Writing for Different Audiences

Prewriting activity. Discuss how audience influences writing. Include such points as vocabulary, tone, style, choice of facts.

Writing assignment. Students pretend that they have been in a car accident and jot down the details of what happened. They then write three letters describing the incident to their parents, to the insurance company, and to a good friend.

John H. Bushman, University of Kansas, Lawrence, Kansas

| DAILY DISCUSSION

When my seniors left my writing class at the end of the semester, I wanted them to take at least two things with them—an ability to find topics to write about on their own and a notebook full of topics that had been explored in class. Both objectives were accomplished, as well as others, through the daily discussion.

The responsibility for the daily, ten-minute discussion rotated around the class, with a different student leading the discussion each day. The leader selected a topic from school, community, national, or world happenings and came to class prepared to provide background information on the topic. Some sample topics might include the following:

> the controversy over where to put the new landfill for the city's garbage
> computer "hackers" who break into private or corporate computer systems
> drugs in professional sports

Presenting background information was to take no more than two to three minutes of the ten-minute discussion. After providing background, the leader asked the class three thought-provoking questions related to the topic. Examples of questions for the topics mentioned above might be:

> How would you react if you learned that the city was proposing to open a new landfill near your home?
> Should computer "hackers" who break into private or corporate computer systems be regarded as criminals?
> What effect, if any, does it have on young people to learn that one of their sports heroes has been disciplined or suspended for drug use?

The class then discussed the questions for the remaining seven or eight minutes. At the end of the discussion time, students recorded the topic and the three questions in their notebooks and then did free-writing on the topic for a few minutes.

To increase the leader's awareness of audience when providing background, two students were selected each day to give feedback to the discussion leader. The two students listed the topic and two or three main points made by the leader when presenting background information. These students' lists were later compared to the discussion leader's own list of main points which was prepared prior to discussion.

During the semester I observed students reading newspapers and magazines, listening to and watching news reports, and tuning in to conversations around them to try to find a topic for discussion. In formulating their questions, they learned to look for key points of an issue, and when presenting their topic, they showed an increasing awareness of their audience by presenting with more clarity the appropriate background. Also their self-confidence in front of the class improved. Finally, as the semester's end approached, I noticed notebooks bulging with topics and realized that many of those topics had, in fact, been the subject of pieces of writing produced during the semester.

Donna Hitchens, Green Bay Area School District, Wisconsin

BITS AND PIECES

Remember placing one hand on a sheet of paper and, with the other hand, tracing around your fingers? This same activity can be enjoyed by high school and college students (especially at the beginning of the year as a get-acquainted exercise), and can prompt both critical thinking and imaginative discussion.

First I ask students to trace their hands on a clean page in their journals. I trace my own hand on the chalkboard while students are tracing theirs. Then I ask students to draw in the fingernails, the scars, the rings, and the knuckles. I explain that, as the next step, we are going to add to our drawings any bits and pieces of information *by which we can be classified*. These bits and pieces might include anything from address, telephone number, and social security number to nicknames, blood type, and the titles of magazines we subscribe to. My own page may include such details as "can do autopsies and CPR," "former Catholic," "chocoholic," "two sons," "Pulsar watch," and "no tonsils, no appendix." I ask students to jot down their words and phrases anywhere on the page, without breaking their information down into categories. Students are to continue writing until the page is full. (Otherwise, they could probably go on ad infinitum.)

The final results contain a fascinating hodgepodge of data, and can be used in several ways in the classroom. One possibility is to ask students to examine the information they've listed and think of contexts in which particular details might be used. For example, a hospital might classify by blood type, a census taker might classify by the number of people in the family, a marketing survey might classify by magazines subscribed to, the post office might classify by address, and so on. Once the more conventional possibilities are exhausted, students are often quite imaginative in coming up with additional ideas.

For certain pieces of information, there might be many possible uses. Students can be asked to select pieces of information that seem especially important and to brainstorm ways in which those facts influence their lives. An address, for instance, is not used only for mail delivery, but determines the school that one attends (or that one's children attend), where one goes to vote, and one's eligibility for free library usage, participation in park district programs, and so on.

If students want to continue in this vein, they might also think of logical ways to group the information on their sheets. There is obviously no correct answer here, and an almost infinite number of possibilities.

As an alternative, students' hand tracings and jottings might be used at the start of the year as a way for students to introduce themselves to one another. Among the details listed, there are bound to be facts that provoke curiosity and discussion and help the class get to know each other better.

James O'Neil, Edison Community College, Fort Myers, Florida

CREATING AN IMPRESSION

In this composition assignment for juniors and seniors, I ask students to write about a person who has made a major impact on their lives. The suggested length is 500 words, and I allow a week for this assignment, broken down as follows.

Day One
Ask each student to think of a person who has made a major positive impact on his or her life, and to brainstorm thirty words that describe this person. Then explain how freewriting works. Ask students to freewrite on all of these topics:

1. Describe an incident or single experience that reveals something about the person you have selected.
2. Write a physical description of this person.
3. Write something that you remember this person saying.

Next, ask students to read through what they have written, noting strong images or perceptive comments. For the following day, ask them to write a more detailed account of an experience based on one of these images.

Day Two
Direct each student to describe his or her person to two classmates. The students listening then ask a total of twenty questions about the described person. This procedure is repeated for each person. After answering his or her classmates' questions, each writer adds notes from this session to a growing "data bank." At this point, ask students to be thinking of one dominant impression.

Day Three
Ask students to jot down answers to these questions:

Have your perceptions of this person changed since you first met him or her? If so, how?

How has this person changed in the time you have known him or her?

What do you think this person will be like five years from now?

What have been the major influences on this person's life?

When and how did you become aware of the influence this person has had on you?

Do you associate this person with a particular place? If so, describe the place.

Do you associate this person with any particular objects or possessions? If so, what are they and why do you associate them with this person?

Has there been a major turning point in this person's life? If so, describe the causes and effects.

Explain to students that they will not be including all of this information in their papers, but only the details necessary to create a single dominant impression. Ask students to have rough drafts ready by the beginning of the next day.

Day Four

Students return to the groups of three in which they worked earlier. In turn, students read their papers aloud once and then exchange papers with the others for a silent reading. Each student then writes letters to the two classmates saying what he or she liked about their papers as well as suggesting improvements.

Day Five

On the last day, students revise their rough drafts with the help of the two letters written by their classmates. I ask students to submit these letters with the final draft and to include a note of their own stating how the suggestions helped them in the revision process.

Marsha Besch, Apple Valley High School, Rosemount, Minnesota

RECORDING A TYPICAL FAMILY MEAL

One summer at the Graduate School of Education of the University of Pennsylvania, I was a member of a class in ethnographic research taught by visiting professor Jeffrey Shultz of Beaver College, Glenside, Pennsylvania.

Dr. Shultz gave us an initial writing assignment that he and his wife, Dr. Janet S. Theophano, have developed for teaching various concepts of ethnographic research. This assignment asked us to write a continuous narrative describing a typical meal at which most and preferably all of our family members were present.

Some of the "guide questions" were:

What was the time of day?
Who was present?
Could you leave early?
Could you start a course before others?
Who prepared the food?
Who served the food?
Who set the table?
Who cleaned up?
What was talked about?
Who did the talking?
Were outsiders ever present?
What role did outsiders play in serving, preparation, cleanup?
Did family members have assigned seats?
Describe the food consumed, the number of courses, and the kinds of
    food included under each course.

This idea struck me as one that we English teachers could use as a writing assignment in our classes. We are always looking for ways to help students develop keen personal voices in their writing. Because of its personal angle, this activity would ensure that all students were working in familiar territory; the necessity of close observation would enhance observation skills and provide

41

a jumping-off point for a discussion of the importance of precision and detail in writing.

This assignment could be used with little revision in the wording of the question list, or it could be used as a model for a question list developed for a different situation. The observing and writing practice provided by such an activity could be valuable for future writing assignments.

Robert H. Rempe, Bishop McDevitt High School, Harrisburg, Pennsylvania

THE $10,000,000 WRITING ASSIGNMENT

Each year, my husband and I are inundated with "junk" mail imploring us to enter various multimillion-dollar sweepstakes. And each year we send in our entries, thinking that, just maybe, this will be *our* year to get rich quick. While discussing what we would do if we won the payload, though, I was amazed at how differently each of us would handle being that wealthy. The almost-heated discussion gave me an idea for a new approach to expository writing with my freshmen.

The $10,000,000 Assignment begins with a discussion of the characteristics of expository writing, concentrating primarily on process writing. Then I pass out mock $10,000,000 checks to the students with their names in the blanks, without even mentioning the assignment. The surprise on students' faces when they receive their checks is delightful. We then discuss the wonderful chore of spending $10,000,000.

At this time, I pass out copies of the following paragraph explaining Assignment 1:

Assignment #1: How to Spend $10,000,000

Congratulations! You are the lucky winner of $10,000,000! That's a whopping $333,000 per year for the next thirty years! To put it another way, that's $27,750 a month, or $6,937.50 a week, or $991.07 a day, or $41.00 an hour, or 68¢ a minute!

Write an expository paper telling the reader how to spend $10,000,000. For prewriting, make a list of items you would buy, charities to which you would donate, and trips on which you would go. Begin your expository paper with an introductory paragraph. Then organize your paper into paragraphs discussing your purchases and your reasons for making those particular purchases. Of course, you'll want a concluding paragraph. Finally, make a collage of all the "things" you could do with $10,000,000.

I give the students the rest of the class period to begin prewriting, look through magazines, and so on. The next day, students complete their expository writings in class and work on their collages, which are due the following day. At that time, students show their collages to the class, and we discuss similarities and differences in their wish lists.

Then I read "What It's Like to Win the Lottery" from the August 1986 edition of *Reader's Digest*, which presents various sides to being an instant millionaire. After discussion, I announce the second assignment, "The $10,000,000 Teen: Is Being a Millionaire Worth It?" and discuss the proper techniques of persuasive writing. Students have two days to complete this assignment and their posters.

Assignment #2: The $10,000,000 Teen: Is Being a Millionaire Worth It?

Write a persuasive essay explaining your views of being ultrawealthy. For prewriting, use the list of material possessions from the first assignment. Then make a second list of the emotional changes you might incur as a wealthy teen. How would family members view you? Try to be realistic and to consider all sides of the issue. Then weigh the two lists and write your persuasive essay discussing why you would or wouldn't like to be a $10,000,000 teen. On the back of your expository collage, make another collage dealing with the emotions expressed in your persuasive paper.

The results of these assignments are fascinating and thought-provoking; while learning the rudiments of process and persuasive expository writing, the students also get a chance to fantasize and search their inner selves.

Kathlyn Hess Arthur, Colorado High School, Colorado City, Texas

THE ROAD MAP
OF LIFE

Each year, students in my sophomore English classes are assigned to write a personal narrative essay. When I approach the class with the assignment, I am filled with excitement. I reminisce to them about the many experiences that I could write about in my own narrative. It's at this point that I realize my students' faces are filled with panic, and I begin hearing comments like, "Nothing exciting has ever happened to me," "I have nothing to write about," and "I can't remember anything that's happened in my life."

After several years of struggling with this problem, I came across "The Road Map of Life," an activity that alleviates students' worries and smooths the way to writing personal narratives.

The goal of this activity is for students to create a "road map" starting at birth and ending at their current age, linking written and illustrated memories, events, and experiences—anything and everything that they want to share about their lives. Creating a road map is an enjoyable experience in itself and also provides a useful foundation for a personal narrative essay. Students can be as creative as they want; they are free to write and draw their maps in any way meaningful to them—jotting or listing names or phrases, writing paragraph descriptions, drawing people, pets, or favorite places, and so on. Some students choose to bring in colored pencils or markers and create marvelously decorated interstate systems that detail a myriad of experiences.

But what is it that gets students to the point of mapping their lives? Since I'm a fan of storytelling, and it's an informal and enjoyable way to share information, I first have students break into groups and tell stories to each other. I simply suggest that they mix and mingle during the class period and ask other members of the class about interesting or memorable experiences from their lives. Throughout these discussions, they jot down ideas for their road maps. Eventually, even the students who protested the most have gathered ideas from their past and present that are possible topics for their narratives.

Not only do my students discover possible topics for their papers, but, by talking out their experiences to others, they move into another stage of prewriting—the brainstorming process. As students remember more details about their stories during discussion, they write them down on their maps.

This helps them later when it comes time to narrow the topic and to cluster ideas for a more structured personal narrative.

I've found this activity to take from one to three class periods, depending on the size of the class. As students share ideas, they see similarities and differences in their lives and get to know one another better. They have a lot of fun explaining their road maps of life to one another, and may even want to display copies on the bulletin board. And it's a great way to generate ideas and create excitement for a personal narrative paper.

Jean Moelter, Turtle Lake High School, Turtle Lake, Wisconsin

100TH-BIRTHDAY WRITING ASSIGNMENT

I often use the 100th-birthday assignment as the first written assignment of the year because it both generates student enthusiasm for writing and helps me get to know students and their interests. However, I'm sure it would be just as effective at any time of year.

I first locate in a current or past edition of the local newspaper a feature story that describes a local person's 100th birthday and life. I distribute photocopies of the story to my students, and we read and discuss it. One story I like to use is about a woman named Marie Rude, who emigrated from Norway at age 19 without knowing a word of English. She worked for $3 a week as a housekeeper, married and had eight children, narrowly escaped death in a tornado, revisited Norway at 85, recovered from a broken hip at 95, and celebrated her 100th birthday by flying over her farm in a private plane. (A teacher whose local paper does not include such features could write a story about the life and 100th birthday of a real or imaginary local person and use it as a model.)

After class discussion, I ask each student to write a newspaper story that might appear on his or her 100th birthday. Students are to include facts from their first fifteen years as well as imagined events from their futures. Many

45

students find it easiest to begin by describing the imagined 100th-birthday celebration and then to review the events of their lives chronologically. With the problems of the beginning and the organization settled, students feel more comfortable writing.

We share rough drafts, revise and edit, and read the final products. Students enjoy writing about that most fascinating topic—their own future—and I learn something about each student's interests, plans, and dreams.

Judy Sheridan, East Grand Forks Senior High School, Minnesota

SEND FOR
THE PRINCIPAL!

Although this assignment was designed as a practice session to help students develop interviewing skills before going out into the community on an oral history project, it also serves as a friendly get-acquainted exercise and an excellent prewriting assignment. Ask your principal to consent to be interviewed by your class about his or her life as a high school student. Students gain experience in preparing leading questions and in following up on details that lead to a good story—and they come to see the principal in a new light.

The list below is typical of the kinds of questions my students asked. They were encouraged to ask follow-up questions on any point as long as the questions were not too personal.

1. Were you the youngest, oldest, or a middle child in your family? What were the advantages or disadvantages of this position?
2. To whom were you closest as you were growing up? Can you remember a special event you both shared?
3. What were the most hallowed rules in your family? Did you ever break any of those rules?

4. Describe the family holiday you most enjoyed. Include activities and food—everything!
5. Describe a typical school day when you were a high school student.
6. How did the atmosphere of your school compare with that of our school? How did the students compare?
7. In what school activities did you participate?
8. What was your greatest moment of triumph in high school and your moment of greatest despair?
9. How did you and your friends spend a typical Saturday night? Describe the night of the "Big Dance."
10. What people or incidents influenced you to seek a career in education?

The class collaborated on writing a lead for their articles on the principal. The material was then presented in order of decreasing importance, according to each student's independent evaluation. This interview and paper were excellent training before students went out into the community to interview, but the fringe benefits—getting to know the principal as a teenager and to perceive that authority in a less stereotyped way—may well have proved as important as my stated objective.

Esther McCune, Glastonbury High School, Glastonbury, Connecticut

FREE WHEELIN' FRED

Among high school students, operating a car is equated with independence and self-expression. This exercise asks students to take a look at personal driving styles and produces lively, imaginative descriptions.

Brainstorm, as a class, the different "driving types": Lead Foot Laurie, Demolition Davy, Low-Ridin' Ralph, etc. Hold a vote to narrow the field to four outstanding choices and ask each student to pick one driving type. Next, students draw pictures of their fictional drivers (nonartists are not penalized; attention to detail is what counts). Each student annotates his or her picture, à la the "Nerd" and "Preppie" posters, using arrows and short blurbs to elaborate on details of the driver's clothes, features, personal habits, etc.

In journals, students expand on their descriptions, providing even more detail: the driver's hobbies, favorite foods, mannerisms, and so on. Each student decides which details to keep and which to eliminate from his or her description and writes a final "driving profile" to be shared with the class.

Dee Chadwick, Flagstaff High School, Flagstaff, Arizona

Scavenger Hunt

A WRITER'S FIELD TRIP

One of the most challenging aspects of teaching composition is formulating topics for student writing—topics which are interesting, enjoyable, and educational for writer and reader alike. Many assignments can become trite and predictable; consequently, the teacher ends up spending hours toiling through compositions that exhibit little in the way of new thought or imagination. These papers are written under duress and follow a standard plan, i.e., "Read the story and explain the symbolism, the theme, the nature of Man. . . ."

"Scavenger Hunt: A Writer's Field Trip" is one activity I have developed that not only makes formulating topics easy, but also provides students with an exercise in honing their observation skills. From the collection process of the field trip, students obtain a wealth of information and ideas that enable them to write essays, short stories, poetry, and dramatic scripts. The range of assignments and activities generated from the "scavenger hunt" is limited only by the imagination, ambition, and daring of the students and the teacher.

The idea came to me when I grew weary of hearing the proverbial "I don't know what to write!" or "I don't know anything to write about!" while teaching sophomore English. What we seemed to need was a collection activity, something to furnish the students with a full load of information. The activity would also need to provide a wide range of composition approaches, thus avoiding the predictability of most assignments.

Through an interest inventory and polling of the class, we discovered that the majority of the students had never been downtown to the heart of the city. Our particular school was one of four high schools in a large suburban setting, some twelve miles from the city center. The school had an enrollment of 1,800 students in grades 9-12, with a low to middle socioeconomic makeup. The student body was culturally and ethnically diverse. Few students had ventured downtown and experienced the beauty and ugliness, the people and rhythms of the city. An excursion into the city seemed to offer a splendid collection opportunity: students would have to use all of their senses for accumulating information.

The old game of a scavenger hunt became the focus of how the students would gather information they could use later in writing. Since cost was an important factor, we decided to use the public transit system: this would be the most inexpensive means of transportation, and would provide the students with excellent opportunities for completing a portion of the scavenger hunt list on their way downtown. (Many students considered this a major event, since they had never ridden a public bus.) The students needed only bus fare and money for lunch, so the school had to cover only the cost of a substitute teacher.

Prior to field-trip day, class time was devoted to interpreting bus schedules, reading and marking maps, and researching facts and features of the city. Teams of two to three students developed sample scavenger items. The students also worked cooperatively in formulating the strategies and rules for the scavenger hunt. They decided that the teams would not see the actual lists until they were on the bus; the instructor would be the only one who knew the items on each list; a three-hour time limit would be set for meeting back at the bus stop once downtown; and the prize for the best team effort and collection would be a day off from class.

The following list provides a sample of the types of information found on the student' lists:

1. List two things that will be in the same place 10 years, 100 years, 1,000 years from today. (State the exact location and give reasons for their stability.)
2. List five things that will be gone tomorrow. (State the exact location and who or what will remove them.)
3. Describe in detail an eyesore. (State the exact location and why the team believes it is an eyesore.)
4. Describe in detail something useless. (Why is it of no use to the team? Who or what might find it useful?)
5. Describe something that needs repair. (How would the team fix it?)

6. Describe something that is being repaired. (How is it being repaired from the team's perspective?)
7. Find at least three examples of a poetic sign, bumper sticker, graffiti, slogan, or advertisement. (What does it say? Does it use imagery, irony, symbolism? Why did it get the team's attention?)
8. Describe in detail a unique individual. (If the team feels comfortable, follow the person for a few minutes, noticing the person's walk, dress, attitude, and gestures. Make up an identity for the individual, i.e., name, family, occupation, education, etc., and attempt a sketch of this individual.)
9. Sketch the most unique building.
10. Sketch the most intriguing/interesting sight other than a human or an animal.
11. Relate/describe examples of kindness, proper etiquette, or caring illustrated by individuals.
12. Relate/describe examples of rudeness or uncaring.
13. Describe a truly bizarre sight, smell, or feeling.
14. Ask four people for directions to a specific location; check their accuracy and how they communicated the instructions, i.e., body movement, vocal intonation, facial expressions, etc.
15. Sit for ten to fifteen minutes in one spot and list all the sounds, smells, feelings, sights, and "tastes" of that location. (Give exact location.)
16. Interview a police officer, valet parking attendant, street cleaner, vendor, street person, hotel door captain, etc. (Formulate some team questions beforehand.)

The students were also given guidelines for possible compositions and assignments that would utilize the information they collected. These guidelines for writing were provided to assist the teams in using their time wisely and to guide their observations so that they would derive maximum benefit for follow-up work in class. They included the following items:

1. *Narrative Essay:* Include personal feelings, impressions, attitudes about the day, the people, the city.
2. *Sensory Images:* Utilizing all the senses, write a descriptive essay about the city for someone who has never experienced an urban area.
3. *Steps in a Process:* Compose a paper speculating on how something is being accomplished or built step-by-step.
4. *Comparison/Contrast:* What are the differences and similarities between the city and your area: the people, daily activities, rhythm, lifestyle, etc.

5. *Short Story:* Several teams combine, and as a group, share the various "characters" they witnessed and formulate a plot using the people and places they observed. Write and illustrate a short story collaboratively.

6. *Drama:* Same as #5, but collaborate on writing a one-act play with all the dramatic elements. Perform the play in class.

7. *Cause and Effect:* Examine a problem viewed by the team and state the cause of the problem and its effects on the city and/or its people.

8. *Research:* Take either the problem in #7 or a new topic and expand it into a research paper, finding sources to support the thesis.

9. *Persuasive Writing:* Similar to #7 and #8, but take a stand on an issue and persuade the reader to take action.

10. *Poetic Interpretation:* Take the sights, sounds, feelings, and rhythms encountered in the city and put the impressions into poetic form.

Initially, this first group of students was somewhat hesitant to participate in the field trip. However, on the bus ride home, they filled the time with one-upmanship stories and shared their reflections on the day. The scavenger hunt became a tremendous motivator in course enrollment, it developed student enjoyment of writing, and it provided me with an entire school year's worth of material for compositions. The students never again uttered, "I don't have anything to write about!"

With a little creative effort by the instructor, the scavenger hunt can be adapted easily to any locale. The idea has been applied to a walking tour of the neighborhood around a school and redesigned to focus on the gathering of the history of a small town. Other teachers have adapted the scavenger hunt idea for their own courses, not only for English but for photography, art history, theater, and science. With adaptation, creativity, and a willingness to try something different, the idea seems to provide an extraordinary, experiential learning activity that students find valuable.

Robert W. Keiper, Western Washington University. Reprinted from Processes and Portfolios in Writing Instruction *(NCTE, 1993).*

Prewriting for

CULTURAL STUDIES COMPOSITIONS

A lot of high school and college composition teachers have begun to include cultural studies assignments in their writing classes. It is commonplace now for composition students to write essays analyzing how magazine or television advertisements achieve their desired effects, how specific places can affect people's behavior, how institutions (schools, churches, corporations, etc.) foster certain beliefs, and how subcultures within those institutions subvert the fostered beliefs. These essays, however, can be difficult for young writers, so I like to precede them with substantive prewriting exercises.

The following exercise for student journals or in-class discussion helps students understand the purpose and methodology of cultural studies before they have to write essays for grades. By examining themselves and their immediate environment as part of a given culture, students begin to gain an understanding of the process of cultural studies assignments.

Journal Assignment
Using this activity as a journal assignment, I usually ask my students to write five or six journal pages, and I allow them two or three days to complete the assignment. I hand out these instructions:

> For this journal assignment, I would like you to complete the following statement: "I am a/an _____." To complete the statement, ask yourself what activity (sport, job, etc.), group (political, social, etc.), or attitude (rebel, conformist, etc.) best defines you as a person.
>
> What do you do that identifies you as a/an _____? Do you like or dislike being a/an _____? What does being a/an _____ mean to you? How would you feel if tomorrow you were no longer a/an _____?
>
> How do other _____s view you? Pick one or two fellow _____s and explain how they perceive you as a/an _____.

How do groups or individuals who aren't _____s view you? Pick one or two people or groups of people who aren't _____s and explain what you think is their perception of you as a/an _____.

In-Class Discussion

Besides providing students with personal insight into the culture around them, this cultural studies prewriting activity is also effective as a topic for in-class discussion. Follow the same organization as the journal assignment. You might even read the journal assignment aloud to your students as a way of prompting discussion. If you suspect that your students may be reluctant to talk about themselves in the public setting of a classroom, you might prearrange to have two or three outgoing students engage in a dialogue with you. You may find that others follow their lead and participate as well.

This prewriting activity helps prepare students for the critical approach they will need to adopt in their graded cultural studies composition assignments. Through this exercise, students begin to understand how social forces influence their lives in both positive and negative ways. Cultural studies assignments are becoming more and more common in high school and college composition classes. I have found that my students' cultural studies essays are much more effective when preceded by prewriting exercises.

Bruce McComiskey, Purdue University, West Lafayette, Indiana

Raiders of

THE LOST ART OF STORYTELLING

The face of Indiana Jones stares at my class from an 8" x 10" glossy photograph. Adventure lurks behind his eyes; narrow escapes permeate every fiber of his sweat-stained fedora. Indiana's picture tells stories. My students tell stories, too—fantastic on-the-spot tales explaining the loss of homework, lateness, or an unexcused absence—yet *writing* stories intimidates them. By using evocative photographs of faces, I help my "raiders of the lost art" enjoy not only the telling but the writing of stories.

I ask students to bring pictures of interesting, startling, or humorous faces cut from newspapers or magazines. To their collection I add pictures I've chosen myself, and we mount each face on a sheet of notebook paper.

Next, I ask students to select from the pictures on the table one face that "speaks" to them. Students may choose the pictures they brought in or different ones. Looking at the chosen pictures, students do a pre-telling using the clustering method below. Students draw the five circles on their papers and write the requested information inside each circle. For each circle in the cluster, students have two minutes to write words and phrases.

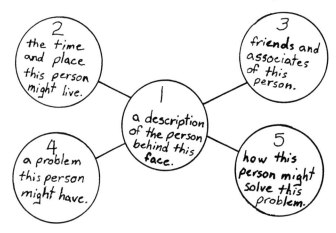

After completing the clustering, students find partners and take turns telling one another the tales suggested by their clusters. Each student has three minutes to tell the story, making any changes he or she wants in the process. The listening student provides feedback as to what he or she likes best and what parts are difficult to understand.

Since stories often change and develop through retelling, students change partners after one telling and tell their stories again, making any changes that they think of. Again students have a three-minute time limit, and listeners must tell the storytellers what they liked and what they found difficult to understand.

At this point it is time for storytellers to become writers. Having told their tales twice, the students can use four minutes to write rough drafts of basic plot lines. Later, students add dialogue, descriptions, and color to stories already well told and tested on an audience.

Sue Frederick, Flour Bluff High School, Texas

GAINING INSIGHTS INTO HUMAN NATURE

My American Literature and Composition class had been working on recognizing the stream-of-consciousness technique which appears in Katherine Porter's "The Jilting of Granny Weatherall." We strained over writings trying to show, not tell. We discussed examples of sensory language from other American literature pieces. Then we read Jerome Weidma's "My Father Sits in the Dark" (Macmillan Literature Series). The in-class discussion was brief, and I feared a short life for the story, the author, and the theme—a fleeting, unsatisfactory outcome. But an idea in the textbook's composition section sparked an idea of my own.

I asked students if they had ever observed someone doing something strange or different from "normal" behavior. Their response was an explosion of such observations: a middle-aged man standing on a street corner doing jumping jacks; an aunt who, on holidays, always reset and rewiped all the dishes on the table; a stranger who danced and sang in front of cars stopped for a traffic light; a grandmother who hoarded food in her bedroom. Some caused laughter; some caused horror; some caused curiosity; some caused concern. The students were hooked.

Next we asked ourselves why people might exhibit such behaviors or habits. But the students who had observed often didn't know. So we examined our responses, brainstormed, reexamined, and created our own theories. Several students decided the man doing jumping jacks could be preparing to run, or maybe he was waiting for his ride to work and used spare time to stay in shape. The aunt was a perfectionist and a nag; "every family has one." The dancing, singing stranger was on drugs or had just gotten a raise or promotion. The grandmother had developed an eating disorder or had Alzheimer's disease and wasn't aware of what she was doing.

The speculations that poured forth showed a clearly developing understanding of fellow human beings. And this insight into human nature fit perfectly into the composition cue: "Write an anecdote—a mere slice of life—about a person the student has observed or invented." We added this: the writer is to show the behavior or habit and, by the end of the piece, reveal why the character behaves as he or she does. It was a perfect opportunity to practice using sensory details, too!

On Day 2 the prewrites were due. Some students had ideas for characters, descriptions, and habits or behaviors, but no reasons for why the characters might be acting in certain ways. So we brainstormed some more and paired up to share ideas.

On Day 3 the first drafts were due. Peer reading groups read, commented, and suggested changes.

On Day 4 revisions were due. Students briefly exchanged revisions to check one another's work for clarity, "showing" rather than "telling," and proper paragraphing. I had the students' undivided attention when demonstrating correct paragraphing and correct use of quotations.

On Day 5 students were to have a draft ready for me to read. Then they had the weekend and a few days to prepare a final draft. These drafts turned out to be remarkable. Not only had the students exhibited a sensitivity to differences of cultures and gender, but they had created rich descriptions of unique characters whom they would earlier have simply labeled "strange" or "different." I believe the students began to sense, too, the limitations of labels, as their thought and discussion led them to a deeper understanding of people's motives and behaviors.

Many of these drafts are less than a page; some are a bit longer. The people are real: an older man who suffers a head injury from storming Normandy; a grandmother who stores vast quantities of food in her room fearing another Depression; a street person who chooses to live there rather than accept societal rules; an aunt whose perfectionism hides her feelings about not having children; a German immigrant who finds safety within the thick walls of an arena basement; a young girl who suffers an eating disorder.

What is particularly exciting is that all my students participated. Students who had previously read the literature with little enthusiasm or hardly attempted the writing assignments, wrote with clarity and perception. We were in their arena—the real world.

Sharon Hexum, Denfeld High School, Duluth, Minnesota

PREWRITING FROM PHOTOGRAPHS

"Things do not change; we change."
—Henry David Thoreau, *Walden*

Upon nearing the conclusion of S. E. Hinton's *That Was Then, This Is Now*, I was eager for my students to look objectively at themselves and to examine changes in their character. Despite the fact that they had eagerly discussed Hinton's characters and their changes, I knew from past experience that classroom discussion involving students' own personal lives and changes would be too risky for some of them. The following assignment resulted in one of our most enjoyable and successful writing projects. The goal was for each student to produce a final paper based on comparison and contrast.

In the introduction to the assignment, I asked my students to reflect upon how they had changed over the years. As I spoke in general terms about the types of changes experienced by teenagers, some students nodded in agreement while others assumed a blank look. It was the second group that would provide the challenge. Next, I asked the students to bring in two photographs of themselves. One should be as current as possible, while the other should be at least three years old but not a baby picture. I explained that a photograph too close to the current one might not illustrate change as well as an older one, and that a baby picture would not be suitable since the student must be able to recall life at the age in the photo.

Almost immediately, a faint murmur of negative comments could be heard. I guessed that some students must consider it uncool to reveal earlier appearances. Therefore, when a few students proclaimed that they had *no* photos of themselves—past or present—I quickly replied that photos were not absolutely necessary, although the students would probably find the assignment easier and more fun if they had them. On the following day, several students who had brought photos displayed them enthusiastically, and others seemed to be watching enviously. The result was that almost everyone brought in photos by the next day. These student photos served three major purposes: to remind students of their past, to focus on a particular time, and to generate interest.

Next, I gave the students a list of statements. This list was the springboard for their final writings, but the students didn't know that yet. Their information sheet was divided into two parts. The top half was titled "That was then," with a place to attach the picture from the past. The bottom half, devoted to the present, was titled ". . . but this is now." Likewise, it included a space for the student's current photo. The response stems for each part follow.

"That was then,"
At age _____, my favorite pastime was . . .
My best friend was . . .
My other friends included . . .
My favorite entertainer was . . .
My room looked like . . .
I wanted to become . . .
When I needed to talk to a parent, I usually went to my . . .
The thing I valued most was . . .
The person I respected the most was . . .
As a student, I was . . .
If I got into trouble, I would . . .
". . . but this is now."
Now, at age_____ , when I have free time I like to . . .
My best friend is . . .
My other friends include . . .
Now my favorite entertainer is . . .
My room looks like . . .
Now my goal is to become . . .
If I need a parent, I would normally go to my . . .
At this time the thing that I value the most is . . .
The person I respect most is . . .
As a student, I am . . .
If I get into trouble, I . . .
Today I am mainly concerned with . . .

By responding to these statements, my students had already collected the details for their papers. At this point, all that remained was the organization. In order to facilitate this, I presented five more statements for completion:

When I was age_____ , I could be described as . . .
Now I can be described as . . .
I can see that I have (or have not) changed in the following ways . . .

My attitude toward life is . . .
I would like to change further (or stay the same) for the following reasons . . .

As soon as the students had reached their conclusions, we discussed the fact that they now had everything necessary to write a well-supported paper regarding changes, or lack of changes, in themselves. I pointed out that in evaluating their papers I would be looking for extensive details from their first group of statements and for substantiated conclusions drawn from their responses to the last group of questions.

Most of the students had eagerly accepted the challenge of this prewriting activity, welcoming and enjoying the chance to reflect on their past, evaluate the present, and even consider the future, somewhat. To their surprise and my delight, the paper writing was easy, they agreed, as a result of the self-examination that they had completed.

The final papers were not displayed, in order to ensure students' privacy, but the prewriting and photos were displayed unless an author objected. Most of the students delighted in reading their classmates' responses and in seeing the photos. This prewriting activity definitely contributed to successful writing; the evidence was completed papers and satisfied writers.

Pat Nance, Oak Ridge High School, Conroe, Texas

IDEA STARTER FOR WRITING A DRAMATIC SCENE

After finishing a drama unit with my ninth graders last year, I was searching for a way to help the students gather ideas for writing plays of their own. Since I had recently planned and attended my parents' Golden Wedding Anniversary, I was newly aware of the wealth of experience which many older people have to share. I decided to ask my students to interview an older person and to use an incident from the interview as an idea starter for a short play or scene—a combination of a *Foxfire* approach with the teaching of genre writing. I gave the following directions:

Interview an older person—a grandparent or someone of your grandparents' generation. Listed below are some ideas for questions to get you started. Add some of your own questions to the list; then pick the ones you want to use. It's up to you how many questions you ask. You might even ask the interviewee to read the questions over and talk about the ones which trigger particular memories. Take notes and get as many concrete details as possible, including what the interviewee wore at the interview and how he or she talked. As the interviewee is talking, try to picture the incidents as scenes in a play.

1. Did you have brothers and sisters? How did you get along? Did you do things together?
2. Did you get into trouble? How were you punished?
3. What kind of games did you play? Did you have special winter games? Summer games? Did you have toys?
4. Did you have birthday parties? Does any one birthday stand out in your mind?
5. Do you remember trying to learn to ride a bike? Who taught you? Was it difficult?
6. Did you have any unusual pets?
7. Who was your best friend? What did you do together?
8. Did you go swimming? Where?
9. Did you ever have any stitches or broken bones?
10. What kind of house did you grow up in? Do you have special memories of one room or one area of the house in which you grew up?
11. Did you have a yard to play in? A fort? A playhouse?
12. Did you have jobs to do around the house?
13. What was your favorite holiday? Did you have any special family holiday traditions?
14. Where did you go to school? How did you get there? Did you ever play hooky?
15. What do you remember about your teachers?
16. Did you go out for sports? Were you involved in many school activities or groups?
17. Did your family go on vacations?
18. Did you ever go to fairs, circuses, or carnivals?
19. Do you remember your first date?
20. What kind of social events did you go to in high school?

21. Who taught you how to drive? What was the first vehicle you drove?
22. Did you work after school?
23. Is there any particular incident or event that you would like to tell about?

Students may find it helpful to work together as they write questions and prepare for their interviews.

After the interviews, I asked the students to bring their notes to class, and I gave them the following instructions:

1. Choose one incident or event from the interview that you can picture as a scene in a play. The incident doesn't have to be terribly exciting, just a "slice of life" from the "olden days," but it will work best if it contains some conflict or drama.
2. You *may* fictionalize your scene. That is, you don't have to stick to the facts. You may add details, characters, and dialogue to make it more interesting. Simply use the ideas from your interview as idea-starters.
3. You may consider this scene as a very short play in itself, or as one scene of a play.
4. Your play should include the following:
    a. a diagram of the stage, description of the set, and explanation of the time and place
    b. a list of characters
    c. stage directions throughout the play, telling where actors walk, how they speak, what they do as they speak

If your scene is only part of a longer play, summarize what happens before and/or after the scene.

Writing plays has always been the most difficult type of creative writing for me to teach, but I have found that this assignment evoked some of the most original and interesting writing I have ever received from my classes. And those students who chose to present their scenes to the class found a receptive and enthusiastic audience.

Barbara Parisien, Cretin-Derham Hall, St. Paul, Minnesota

RADIO THRILLS AND CHILLS

My sophomores were finding it difficult to relate to Howard Koch's 1938 radio play *Invasion from Mars*. Students seemed baffled and yet intrigued at how this play could send a rush of panic through the citizens of New York. Thus, to extend and synthesize their knowledge of the play, I ask my students to come up with their own radio play designed to send terror through citizens of our day and time.

Students seem apprehensive at first, not knowing exactly what kind of an event to plan for. We begin brainstorming events on the board. I ask them to think of events that would cause them to panic if they were to hear an announcement interrupting a program on the radio. Some ideas volunteered have been:

- a major weather disaster (tornado, hurricane, flood, etc.)
- a national epidemic (or the water supply infected with a deadly bacterium)
- the total depletion of the ozone layer
- a killer Santa Claus
- a major nuclear war

Students work in groups and use these ideas to create their own radio plays. I usually give them the following handout to guide them through this process. I also use this guide as a rubric when grading the projects.

"An Invasion"

1. Choose a disaster or event that might send a panic across our nation as *Invasion from Mars* did in 1938.
2. Decide what type of radio station you are going to be. Give your radio station a name.
3. Write the script for your disaster. This should be edited and turned in when the radio program is finished.
4. Choose music fitting for both your station and your event. Remember, be creative; humor and good use of sarcasm are permitted.

5. Be prepared to record. Someone needs to bring in a blank audiocassette tape on which to record.

Once the plays have been written, edited, and recorded, each "station" goes "on the air" to thrill the classroom audience.

This assignment allows for much creativity, broadens the students' understanding of Koch's play, and gives them a better understanding of writing dialogue. The students love the assignment and the opportunity to "create" a disaster!

Karen Jackson, North Laurel High School, London, Kentucky

RETURNING TO FAIRY TALES

Fairy tales and folk tales aren't just for children anymore. They offer adults and young adults a means to recapture some of the delights of childhood, and also offer students out-of-the-ordinary material for a study of some of the aspects of literature.

Fairy tales, folk tales, and other stories that fall into this genre are the basis of much of the literature of our various cultures. Themes from such stories appear over and over again in poems, plays, novels, and modern television and movies. The so-called Cinderella story, for example, has been a favorite of romance writers since romances were first written.

In this unit, students explore their favorite fairy tales and folk tales, write their own stories, and then analyze, in a scholarly fashion, a well-known story. My hope is that in using this material the students will learn the process of analysis through a medium that is entertaining and familiar as well as instructional.

Step One
To introduce this unit, I asked students what kinds of stories they read or had

read to them as children. Many titles were brought up, and we noted that many of the stories beloved by children were enjoyed by the adults who were reading them aloud. To the fairy tale titles that came up, I added a few that I remembered particularly well from my own childhood.

Students brought up the prevalence of Disney movies made from popular fairy tales and the fact that the film *Beauty and the Beast* had recently started playing in our town. This opened our discussion of the fact that there have been many versions of this story and of other fairy tales, in both books and films. I mentioned several other versions of this particular tale, and we scanned some of the material written about fairy tales in *Spells of Enchantment: Wondrous Fairy Tales of Western Culture* (Viking, 1991). It might also be useful to assemble a few collections of fairy tales from other cultures, in case students would like to browse. The Time-Life series *The Enchanted World*, available in some public libraries, is one possible resource for international tales.

I showed students various editions of fairy tales from different publishers, including editions from Golden Book and Disney and others intended for older readers. We noted that, although the same story may vary from book to book, the general idea of the story remains the same. I referred students interested in further research to Bruno Bettelheim's *The Uses of Enchantment: The Meaning and Importance of Fairy Tales* (Random, 1989).

Step Two
Students wrote their own stories, either alone or with a partner. They wrote a first draft, which was read aloud to the class for suggestions, comments, and criticism. They completed a final draft including illustrations, covers, and so on. For this exercise I did not read or correct first drafts.

Step Three
As a class, we discussed the fact that fairy tales have been studied and interpreted in many different ways. I gave students copies of a movie review of the film *Beauty and the Beast*, in which the reviewer examines different versions of the story and the ways in which it has been treated in both books and films. (Relevant reviews of this film and of the Disney film, *Sleeping Beauty*, should still be available in back issues of newspapers and news magazines.)

Step Four
Working individually, students selected a well-known fairy tale, preferably an illustrated version, and wrote an essay of analysis. They had the option of selecting one of their favorites or choosing from one of the collections in the classroom.

Students were asked to make a careful reading of the selected work and, in their essays, to address aspects that might be relevant for their analysis. A partial list of possible questions to be addressed is shown below.

What is the theme or main idea of the book?

Is the theme a familiar one that has appeared elsewhere? If so, where? (Other media—television, movies, comic books, etc.—may be included.) Compare and contrast the treatments.

What is the tone of the story?

What kinds of language does the author use?

What types of figurative language or literary devices appear in this story?

How do the illustrations enhance or add to the effectiveness of the story?

How is the conflict or problem in the story resolved?

Does the story attempt to provide the reader with a moral lesson?

Will the characters live happily ever after? If so, why?

Conclude your essay by giving your opinion on why the appeal of such stories/books has lasted so long, and why they are constantly in print.

The students were free to research additional information in the library, or to base the paper entirely on their own opinions, observations, and knowledge. The organization of the material was up to each student; however, students were asked not to merely answer the questions posed but to arrange the material in a formal essay.

Students enjoyed taking part in this in-depth look at fairy tales, and learned firsthand that not all stories read to children are strictly children's stories.

To conclude the unit, we watched and discussed the film version of Sondheim's play "Into the Woods," which synthesizes elements from well-known folk tales into an original story. This made an excellent and entertaining finale to our fairy tale project.

Sally Hellman, Las Vegas High School, Las Vegas, Nevada

GARBOLOGY EXERCISE

B efore my freshman honors class begins a unit on reading short stories, we spend several weeks writing them. I focus a great deal on characterization and on writing indirect characterization. One of the students' favorite activities is what I call the Garbology Exercise.

The day before we use this exercise, we read an excerpt from John Steinbeck's *Travels With Charley* (Bantam, 1975, pp. 115-119). The brief excerpt is about a hotel Steinbeck stays in; he arrives early and his room is not ready. Since he is tired from traveling, he simply states that he will sleep in the hotel lobby until the room is ready. The hotel management, not wishing to have a scroungy-looking man sleeping in the lobby even if he *is* John Steinbeck, arranges to have Steinbeck stay in a room that has not been cleaned until his own room can be readied. In this room Steinbeck forgets his weariness as he finds numerous clues to the room's previous occupant by examining the garbage left behind. He pieces together the life of Lonesome Harry by sifting through his discarded notes, cigarettes, antacid wrappers, and so on. Students love this amusing story, and they enjoy observing Steinbeck's investigation in progress. We discuss Steinbeck's conclusions about Harry and how he creates an interesting character from nothing more than garbage.

The next day the students come to class prepared, like Steinbeck, to become amateur "garbologists." I have already explained that garbology is a field of archeology in which the scientist goes through the garbage of a culture and draws conclusions about the lives of the people. Before we begin, I tell them to divide their paper in half vertically; on the left-hand side they will inventory the items, and on the right-hand side they will write their conclusions about the person or persons based on their evaluation of the garbage. I caution them to leave the garbage as they have found it; if a magazine is open to a certain page it must be left open to that page! If a note is crumpled up, it can be smoothed out to be read, but it must return to the pile crumpled up. Second, there must be no talking or sharing of ideas. Sharing ideas would only prejudice others. If a student misses an important clue, so be it. The object of this exercise is to allow the observers to draw their own, individual conclusions.

The "garbage" is made of things I have gathered from around my own home. Of course, it is "clean" garbage—primarily paper products, empty aspirin bottles, and so on. The students know that the "owner" or "owners" of this trash are fictional characters created by their own minds, and that there are no right or wrong conclusions.

The next step is for students to write a story about this person or persons. Students' stories are to be based on what they have deduced from their garbology observations, and must include the mention of at least one item in the garbage.

Since students spend time studying evidence of the person's lifestyle and habits before they write, the resulting stories tend to be inventive and to show strong characterization. With this creative preface, my students, or garbologists, as they like to refer to themselves, are prepared to read assigned narratives with an analytical eye.

Evelyn I. Funda, Kofa High School, Yuma, Arizona

STRONG CHARACTERS PRODUCE LIVELY DIALOGUES

Creating a dialogue between characters can be a difficult assignment for students. Adequate preparation helps my students develop lively, interesting dialogues.

Before any writing is assigned, I read aloud two or three rich character descriptions from literature. Students are to imagine what the person being described is actually like. (After hearing Washington Irving's description of Ichabod Crane, one student volunteered to draw a portrait on the chalkboard.)

Next, I ask a student to suggest an occupation so that we may do a class composite character sketch.

"Truck driver," Dexter offers.

"How old is this truck driver?" I ask Antoinette.

"Forty-five."

"Male or female?" I ask.

"Female," the class decides.

"What does she look like?" I point to Charles.

"She's tall, with flaming red hair."

We continue until a thorough (and usually pretty comical) character is created. At this point, each student draws from a hat a slip of paper on which a general character description is written, such as a preschool teacher or a television repair person. Other characters that I have used are listed below:

Midwestern farmer	rock star
subway driver	comedian
waitress	fortune teller
construction worker	reggae drummer
talking dog	escaped convict
precocious four-year-old	creature from Venus
football player	grandmother
stockbroker	preppy college student
Broadway dancer	brain surgeon
arrogant poet	absent-minded professor
preacher	hair dresser
politician	psychologist

There is a different character on each slip. The students have ten minutes to write a description of their characters. I caution students to avoid stereotypes or derogatory remarks. Rather, they are to search for details that make their particular character unique.

One class instituted the next step, which has become a favorite part of the activity. Each student reads his or her description aloud while the rest of the class tries to guess the identity of the character. This activity encourages students to write vivid descriptions, to show rather than to tell.

Next we put the character sketches aside and discuss setting. Again, I read descriptive settings from literature, and students guess where and when the scene takes place. The hat is passed around once again, and this time I've listed particular settings on the slips of paper, such as the following:

deserted island	noisy discotheque
crowded bus	synagogue
our high school	ship at sea
top of Washington	battlefield
Monument	French café
school cafeteria	elevator

haunted house	delivery room
private plane	prison cell
empty cornfield	undiscovered planet
lion's cage	

I list the same setting on two slips of paper, so that two students will pick "haunted house" or "French café." Students write for ten minutes describing their settings.

Now the fun begins. I ask the students to call out their settings and to pair up with the other student who has the same setting. Each twosome now has two characters and one setting in which to create a dialogue. My only instructions are to write two pages of dialogue between the two characters, trying to introduce a conflict in the dialogue that will gain and hold the audience's attention. My students know that they will read their dialogues aloud to the class, and so far all have created lively, entertaining dialogues.

Jill M. Weiler, McKinley High School, Washington, D.C.

THE ART OF PERSUASION

I thought my eleventh-grade vocational students might take a cue from Puritan minister Jonathan Edwards's "hellfire and brimstone" sermon, "Sinners in the Hands of an Angry God."

As I read through an excerpt from this sermon in our English text, I was struck by the focus on persuasion in this selection. Since modern day teens are bombarded daily by persuasive techniques on television and radio and in magazines and newspapers in the form of advertisements, I devised a two-day lesson to convey the importance of persuasive techniques.

I began by writing the word *persuasion* on the board and asking students what the word means. "Convincing someone to do something" was a particularly good response. Next we moved to a discussion of the types of persuasion that students are most familiar with—the persuasive techniques that they recognize in printed and visual advertising. I cited the example of an advertisement for donations to relief organizations in developing countries that used a photograph of malnourished children with sad, sunken eyes, and bulging stomachs. Students recognized that such advertisements used an appeal to emotions.

Next, students looked through magazines for examples of advertisements using other types of appeals.

Typical examples included advertisements which implied that a product could make someone attractive to the opposite sex; that an admired celebrity used a particular product; and that the user of a certain product would have more fun. In the ensuing discussion, students returned to the point that the purpose of persuasion is to change someone's behavior.

Then it was time to take a look at Jonathan Edwards's sermon. I read the sermon aloud to the students, who recognized that fear was the appeal that Edwards used. They also noted that the Puritans hearing his sermon were uncertain whether they would, in fact, have a rewarding afterlife. At this point, I asked students to think of school-related issues involving behaviors or situations that they would like to change—issues that might allow us to try out some of the persuasive techniques we'd discussed. These ideas were due the following day.

The next day we briefly discussed persuasive techniques, and I read aloud an editorial from our local newspaper as another example of an attempt to persuade someone. We talked about the importance of a "reasonable and convincing tone" when using persuasion. Students then turned to their examples of school-related behaviors that they might be able to influence. They were eager to present their examples, suggesting such topics as the serving of non-nutritious food in the school cafeteria, the creation of a smoking lounge for students, and the rule prohibiting students from leaving the school building for lunch. Students decided to focus on the issue of being able to leave the school grounds at lunchtime.

I explained that students were to write a persuasive petition about the lunchtime rule. At first they identified fellow students as their intended audience, but then they realized that it was the school administration and the school board that they would need to convince.

As a group, the class wrote a rough draft of a petition to the school authorities. We discussed concerns and reservations that the board might raise, and students came up with counterarguments. Then students revised their original draft.

The final argument was in the format of a petition addressed to the school principal. Each student was to secure signatures on a copy of the petition. When sufficient signatures had been gathered, I presented the petitions to the principal, who later visited our classroom to discuss the issue further. He emphasized to the class that he was impressed by their attempts to put their desires into writing and by their presentation of arguments. He told the students that he was unable to make a decision on the matter, but that he would discuss the petition with the school board.

As of this writing, the students are waiting for the school board's response. But whatever the outcome may be, I know that students have come to understand persuasion as a literary device, and appreciate the importance of persuasive techniques.

Paula J. Campbell, Northampton Area Senior High School, Northampton, Pennsylvania

Might versus Right
DORIS LESSING'S "NO WITCHCRAFT FOR SALE"

Gideon, the central character in Doris Lessing's compelling short story "No Witchcraft for Sale," evokes powerful discussion and more powerful writing from my ninth-grade interdisciplinary humanities students. The African's refusal to impart his knowledge of herbal medicine to his white employers, although he has earlier used it to save their son's eyesight after a snake attack, raises challenging questions of cultural difference and power in human relationships.

Our humanities course integrates art and music with the core English and social studies curricula, focusing on the theme of goodness in people, life, and society. The New York State emphasis in the ninth-grade social studies program is on the Middle East, Africa, South Asia, and the Pacific Rim. Over the past decade we have found several works, in a variety of genres, that help the students understand the cultures and histories of parts of each of these important areas. Two full length works by women authors, for example, are currently included in the readings: *Many Waters*, by Madeline L'Engle, and *Nectar in a Sieve*, by Kamala Markandaya.

Lessing's incomparable skill at presenting a values controversy in her short story is evidenced by the fact that students vividly remember the story years later. I begin the discussion by introducing the author and her commitment to human rights and human dignity. Next the students read the story silently, making notes if there are any passages they do not understand, or if there are ideas or attitudes they wish to discuss later. After reading the story, students record their reactions in their journals.

When the students have completed their reading and responding, I initiate a discussion by asking the students to vote on Gideon's decision to withhold his knowledge from his employers and from the pharmaceutical company. Invariably the vote is dramatically in Gideon's favor. The underdog has triumphed over the tyrant. We then discuss the elements of the story, as Lessing presents it, that led us to our decision.

Students next assume the persona of one of four characters from the story and write in their journals. Each student (a) describes the incident from the character's point of view; (b) explains how that character felt about the decision; and (c) justifies that character's opinion from the evidence given by the author and from the student's own knowledge of circumstances in that society.

Students next move into "persona groups" to share their reactions and to test the ideas they've written down in terms of accuracy and voice.

They then shift into groups in which all the personas are represented. Again they share their responses. To develop a fuller understanding of the different points of view, each student also paraphrases the feelings of the character on the left. Groups share any problems they are not able to resolve.

We return to large-group discussion and examine what transpired in the course of the group discussions. I end class by asking the students to prepare a journal entry for the following day in which they discuss the story in terms of the course theme of what defines "goodness" in persons, life, and society.

The students are finally able to use the discussions and their journal entries as the source of an extended essay in which they compare Gideon with two characters they have met earlier in the course: Kunta Kinte from Alex Haley's *Roots* and Stephen Kumalo from Alan Paton's *Cry the Beloved Country*.

Students spend several days preparing their rough drafts, after which they share their drafts in peer response groups, take time to revise them, edit them, return to groups, and finally present their finished essays. Each group presents to their social studies teacher one essay chosen from their group.

Joan A. Droit, Grand Island High School, Grand Island, New York

One Writer to Another

AN APPROACH TO "YOUNG GOODMAN BROWN"

Young Goodman Brown" poses the kinds of problems that respond well to a teaching method based on creative writing. Hawthorne's diction is difficult for my students, his theme is troublesome, and if the anthology we're using mentions the terrifying word *symbolism* in presenting the story, many of my students decide at the outset that they'll never "get it." However, two writing projects have helped them enjoy the story and have rewarded me by provoking vigorous classroom discussions.

The first writing assignment is groundwork. I ask the students to close their eyes as I set the scene for them:

> You are on the tenth floor of a tall building and have entered the elevator. The door closes and the elevator starts going down. You watch the lights marking the floors: 10, 9, 8 . . . . The motion is slow. At the ground floor, the door opens onto a hallway. You walk toward a door and open it to find yourself in the world's most peaceful setting. Observe the scene in all its detail, keeping your eyes closed throughout.

A minute of this silent observation seems like a long time, and after about that long I ask students to open their eyes and to write down what they seemed to see, hear, touch, taste, or smell in their imaginary spaces. Even the reluctant students settle down despite disavowals, and everybody writes something.

Then I lead them through this exercise again, this time taking them to the world's most terrifying place and asking them to describe it in writing when they open their eyes. The commotion is delightful; everyone has a lot to write for this one, and many are sorry to have to part with their papers before they're finished. We all get up and stretch, and in pairs we trade observations about the classroom or the view out the window for a minute to bring us back to our shared reality. For the rest of the class period we discuss something else.

After class I read the descriptions (no quibbles about grammar, organization, etc.) and chart the motifs. While each group of students presents its own constellation, one typical chart looks like this:

Category	Peace	Terror
Natural settings	woods, park, beach (4), island, sea (3), lake, sun (8), clear sky (7), cool water, dew, breezes (2), soft clouds, birds (5), squirrels, horses (2), butterflies, grasses, flowers	forest (2), valley, desert, sea, night (3), other darkness (4), stormy waves, wind (2), dark clouds (2), bees, dogs, monsters, snakes, bare trees (2), cliffs
Other settings, details	heaven, clean room, dining room, living room, bedroom, candle-light, food (3)	subway, pit, cave, small room, highway, hospital, graveyard, deathcamp, battleground, ax, knife, door, cage
Miscellaneous	warmth (3), cool-ness (2), bird songs (3), rustlings, calm voices, sunset, blue (3), gold (4), food smells	warmth, burning (2), cold (2), chaotic noises (3), roar, crying (2), screams, groans, gray (2), black, murky colors, sweat, burning flesh smells
Feelings	rich (2), smart, floating on sea, on air, being in love (3), ecstacy, timelessness	helpless (4), threatened (11), falling (2), being punished, pursued (4), trapped (2), lost (2)

74

| Social setting | lover (2), wedding, family (4), children (3), solitude (2) | assailant, demon, dead people (2), strangers, alone (4), abandoned |

(Note: The numbers in parentheses show how many students used the image. No number means that only one student used it.)

During the next class period, we discuss the chart. (Alternatively, true to the spirit of writing across the curriculum, we might sharpen students' classification skills by presenting them with the raw count of random entries and asking them to compose the categories and formulate generalizations.) Students are often surprised to see that other people share what they thought was a unique image, and this moves us toward a discussion of archetypes. Even more lively are the arguments about how warmth (for instance) can be part of one's image of peacefulness, but part of another person's image of terror. This leads to questions about what makes a system of images internally coherent as well as evocative of themes beyond itself. Usually I am not the first to use the word *symbolism* and by the time the word surfaces, the concept is fully familiar.

The reading of "Young Goodman Brown" profits in several ways. Many students are intrigued to find Hawthorne's imagery overlapping with their own or with the group's composite—overlapping despite a century's difference in perspective. Dark forests, snakes, fire, and human tumult are all touchstones by now. Some students, through the writing exercise, have caught on to the double vision of figurative language, a skill that opens up their responses to Hawthorne's irony as well as to his allegory. And, finally, everyone is interested in the narrator's question at the end: "Had Goodman Brown fallen asleep in the forest and only dreamed a wild dream of a witch-meeting?" Having gone down their elevators right in the middle of class, students recognize that dream and reality are not polar opposites and that imaginative activity can reach from one mode of consciousness to another. That Goodman Brown's perceptions in the forest that night should alter the rest of his life no longer seems preposterous, though it may continue to be troubling.

There's more to "Young Goodman Brown" than imagery, of course, and once students have something to hold on to, they feel freer to explore the thematic and structural questions. Some of those explorations have yielded better fruit than others, but I have always been pleased with the results of the second creative writing project I offer in our study of "Young Goodman Brown." In my list of suggested topics for midterm essays, I include this:

Rewrite the ending of "Young Goodman Brown" from the point where Goodman cries "Faith! Faith! . . . look up to heaven, and resist the wicked one." Change the outcome in some significant way

75

but try to maintain the tone, style, and narrative point of view of the original story. When you're through, attach a paragraph or two discussing the problems you encountered and any thoughts about how you've changed the theme.

Since the students can choose to write on some other topic or other work, those who choose this topic are either the ones who have thought carefully about "Young Goodman Brown" or the ones who like to write. Consequently, the results often show great care.

But even the weaker papers provide excellent opportunities for the class to look one last time at the issues in Hawthorne's story. My students are used to having their papers read by classmates in a peer-critiquing process, and they often work on revisions in small groups, so by midterm most are happy to read their essays to the class. Goodman's changes of destiny at the hands of my students have been by turns hilarious, poignant, nihilistic, bourgeois, outrageous, tragic, and melodramatic, but they have always been fascinating. The writers have confronted difficult questions of craft and emerged with a fresh respect for Hawthorne (often a reversal of a previous attitude). Their classmates have framed criticisms about plausibility, unity, and style. For my part, I have enjoyed sitting in a corner and cheering as they worked together toward the formulation of some ideas as insightful and eloquently expressed as the best I could hope to offer them from the lectern.

Evelyn Farbman, Greater Hartford Community College, Hartford, Connecticut

TELLING STORIES, PROMPTING MEMORIES

A goal of our English curriculum is to integrate reading, writing, and speaking instruction. In English II, the students begin the year by reading *I Am the Cheese*, which is followed by a narrative essay assignment. The activity explained below is a way of integrating skills by using themes of the novel and storytelling to brainstorm essay topics.

First, I ask students to come to class prepared to share a personal experience relating to one of the themes of the novel. For *I Am the Cheese*, I give students the option of explaining either a time they felt fear or a time they wanted to seek revenge. When they come to class, we move our desks into a circle. I begin by telling the students about coming upon an accident that my father had when I was in high school, asking them to list any of their own experiences that come to mind as they listen to my story. I also tell them that even though we are sharing stories relating to fear or revenge, the experiences on their lists need not be limited to these emotions. Proceeding around the circle, each student tells his or her story, and the other students list experiences that come to mind.

The power of association is amazing. Often students will exclaim, "Oh, I remember when . . . ," as hearing a story leads them to recall some long-ago incident. This year, while one student told of having a "chicken fight" on monkey bars with a girl wearing clogs when they were in grade school, another girl cried, "Oh, in fourth grade I ran away from home because my mother wouldn't buy me a pair of clogs."

By the time we make our way around the circle, students have a wealth of personal experiences they could use as topics for a narrative essay. We then discuss how to determine which potential topics would be best for the assignment.

I have found this method of brainstorming effective for several reasons. First, as the students think of a story to share with the class, it helps them to make connections between their own lives and the themes of the novel. Also, if used at the beginning of the year, this activity provides a nonthreatening first speaking experience that the students really enjoy. Finally, as a brainstorming tool, it enables students to retrieve some wonderful stories they might not have been able to recall otherwise.

Kimberly K. Austin, Community High School District #94, West Chicago, Illinois

BRITISH LITERATURE FREEWRITINGS

I assign a variety of different writings and essays in my British literature class, but one thing is always the same no matter what author we are reading or what the major writing assignment is. I always introduce a writing assignment with five minutes of freewriting.

Freewriting gives students a more relaxed attitude toward the writing process and allows them to probe their imaginations on a topic related to the reading. It makes their later writings both more fluid and more creative.

I allow students five minutes to write without lifting their pens from the paper. I often provide a role model by writing along with my students; when students volunteer to read their writings, I read mine also.

Here are examples of topics I might suggest to accompany specific works:

Beowulf—Describe your idea of a hero or heroine.

Chaucer's "Prologue" to *The Canterbury Tales*—Imagine that you are on a pilgrimage to Canterbury and record your impressions.

Shakespeare's "Sonnet 130"—What is your idea of beauty?

Swift's *Gulliver's Travels*—Describe what you would do if you, like the inhabitants of Brobdingnag, encountered a person only five or six inches high.

Dickens's *A Tale of Two Cities, David Copperfield,* or *A Christmas Carol*—Create a vivid character description and give your character a memorable name.

Yeats's "The Lake Isle of Innisfree"—Picture a place that is your ideal of natural beauty and describe it.

Wells's *The Time Machine*—Write a description of what you find on journeying to a future world.

Saki's "Tobermory"—Imagine that you have just discovered that a family pet can talk, and write the dialogue that takes place between you two.

Frank O'Connor's "My Oedipus Complex"—Write a description from the point of view of a five year old. For example, you could describe where you live, describe what you do when you get up in the morning, or describe an event like riding the bus or meeting a strange dog.

An imaginative teacher will not have difficulty devising topics to complement other literary works. There are many advantages to the practice of using freewritings, from increased participation in discussions to increased confidence in writing.

Sr. Mary Crepeau, Bishop Connolly High School, Fall River, Massachusetts

CHARTING CHAUCER'S CHARACTERS

Using a chart to analyze a text, I taught my senior basic English students how to recognize and identify methods of characterization in literature and then to apply similar methods in their own writing.

After I read aloud excerpts from Chaucer's "Prologue" to *The Canterbury Tales*, we discussed the numerous ways that Chaucer developed the characters, narrowing these character attributes to the following three for analysis: physical descriptions, personality traits, and actions. The students read the selection silently, and then constructed their own chart. An example of a completed chart appears on page 81.

This assignment encouraged more than just literal comprehension of a text. To construct the chart, students had to analyze, classify, organize, differentiate, and interpret. With the text graphically organized, it became apparent to the students that descriptive details created vivid images and, thus, memorable characters.

Students were now ready to write a characterization. Using listing as a prewriting technique, students looked for people in their own lives whom they could characterize. Reviewing the chart shown above, with its three different methods of characterization and the details included in each, helped students as they created word pictures to describe their characters. During the revision process students prepared similar charts from their own writing. This was an invaluable step in showing students the methods and details they used in their characterizations and helping them evaluate their own writing.

Joan Meharg, Round Rock High School, Austin, Texas

Charting Chaucer's Characters

	Physical Appearance	Actions	Personality Traits
Knight		Fought 15 wars in foreign countries	Loved code of chivalry: honor, truth, freedom, courtesy Not rude Respected each man's right Wise Prudent Meek Shunned vileness
Squire	Curly hair 20 years old Wore short embroidered gown with long, wide sleeves	Fought courageously in Flanders, Artois, and Picardy Sang Played flute Rode horses well Wrote songs Stayed up late singing love songs	A merry blade Lover full of fire Active Bright Strong Humble Courteous
Prioress	Straight nose Transparent gray eyes Small, soft red mouth Wide forehead Wore well-designed cloak, coral and green beads with an engraved gold brooch on arm	Sang sweetly through her nose Spoke French Fed her dogs the best food	Well-mannered Amiable Liked jokes Interested in latest fashion at court Soft-hearted

Mapping
A PREWRITING TECHNIQUE THAT WORKS

Every writer begins by facing a blank page, waiting for ideas and words. Some writers make lists before writing, some work out ideas in their minds, some outline, some doodle—but all writers develop techniques for beginning. Mapping is one such technique. Because it helps writers generate ideas, because it allows them to add or delete material readily, and because it is easily learned, mapping is an extremely useful skill.

WHAT IS A MAP?

A map is a graphic representation of a written or oral composition; often it includes only key words. It adds a visual dimension that helps students gain greater control of and fluency in thinking and writing. A map helps students produce and receive information, organize that information, and go on to create a product uniquely their own. Because it teaches students to differentiate among primary, secondary, and tertiary ideas, a map aids composing and comprehending. Mapping can be a prewriting, revising, or postwriting activity, enabling students to organize, compose, and evaluate their writing.

INTRODUCING MAPPING

Introduce mapping to students with an everyday topic that allows them to work together to generate an extensive list of related words and ideas. This step does not differ significantly from what is often called brainstorming. With junior high students I have used such topics as sports or soap; with high school students such topics as advertising or the troubles of being seventeen. Writing about a best friend or what-if topics (What if no adults came to school today?) are also good choices.

When students seem to have run out of ideas, we organize the words into

82

categories. At this step students frequently get new ideas and insights as they begin to perceive a structure that can be expanded or contracted depending upon the writer's purpose and intent. The topic *soap*, for example, yielded the following terms and categories:

type	*use*	*color*	*smell*	*texture*
liquid	shower	white	fresh	gritty
powdered	bath	green	lemon	granule
bar	dishes	pink	clean	slippery
	clothes	yellow	herbal	bubbly
	laundry	creamy	bayberry	sudsy
	cleaning	milky	spicy	satiny
	cars	iridescent	outdoorsy	creamy
	lubricant		pine	fluffy
	blowing bubbles		floral	smooth

Next, students arrange these categories and words on a map like the one shown below, with the controlling topic or idea in a dominant position and the supporting ideas as extensions. A pinwheel shape, however, is only one of the many configurations that will develop. Again, new ideas often emerge during mapping and additions and deletions should be encouraged. At this step, mapping encourages interaction among students, and these interchanges help to prepare students to write their own essays later on.

83

Based on our map, we work out a topic sentence as a group and draft a first paragraph together before students take off on their own to complete their drafts. We revise these in small groups, and read some to the class and show others on the overhead projector.

After an introduction to mapping, students typically go on to create more individualistic maps. Older students develop relatively sophisticated ones (interlocking triangles, concentric circles, ladders) that help them structure their writing and shape it for special purposes and audiences. Mapping in a sense provides its own outline—each category inviting development with explanation, definition, classification, example, narration, comparison.

MAPPING A MORE COMPLICATED ASSIGNMENT

Mapping a short story or essay before writing about it helps students discern how an author has structured ideas. The example below illustrates how a fifteen-year-old sophomore was able to show parallels between Chaucer's "Knight's Tale" and his "Miller's Tale"—first by mapping, then in writing a first draft of a comparison paper. Clearly, the mapping technique assisted this student in writing a draft that both analyzes and synthesizes the structures of the two tales.

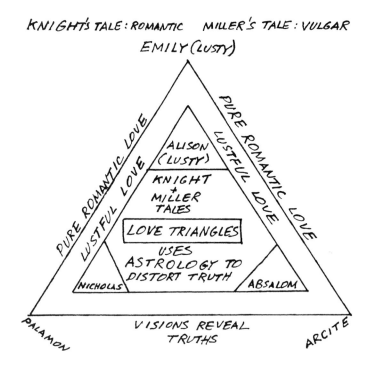

A Comparison of the Knight's Tale and the Miller's Tale

After the knight finished his beautiful (and overlong) tale, everyone agreed it was noble. The drunken miller, however, thought he could match any tale of the knight's. At first, the two tales seem to be totally opposite, but after a closer look one can find many similarities.

Both tales involve a love triangle, where two men seek the love of the same woman and fight for her. In "The Knight's Tale" the characters are Palamon, Arcite, and Emily. In "The Miller's Tale" the characters are Absalom, Nicholas, and Alison. The knight's triangle is very pure and romantic. The miller's triangle is somewhat raunchier; Nicholas, for example, had already won Alison while Absalom was still begging for her love.

Visions are used in both tales. Palamon, Arcite, and Emily pray to the gods in an effort to guide their destiny, and Emily sees a vision of the goddess Diana. In the miller's tale visions are mocked. Nicholas also uses visions in an effort to guide his destiny—or his and Alison's. He pretends to have seen a vision from the gods, telling him a great flood is coming, to trick the carpenter into hiding in a barrel.

Destiny solved the differences between Palamon and Arcite. Both men won, even though Arcite died. He won Emily's hand in marriage and then had an accident. As he lay dying, he gave Emily to Palamon. So it was in the miller's tale; everyone was "rewarded" so to speak: foolish Absalom with a misplaced kiss, over-confident Nicholas with a severely burned bottom, and the anxious carpenter with a broken arm.

The miller took almost every detail of the knight's tale and twisted it into something vulgar so that the stories seem to be very dissimilar. However, after careful scrutiny, many likenesses can be found. As a matter of fact, both stories parallel each other.

CONCLUSION

Mapping enhances verbal thinking because it provides a visual/spatial perspective, allowing poorer writers to generate and shape ideas with greater ease and assisting more sophisticated writers with analysis and synthesis. Mapping seems to be effective because it combines what Susanne Langer called the discursive (speaking, listening, reading, and writing) with the presentational (art, music, dance, and sculpture)—two basic ways we symbolize experience. By using both the verbal and the spatial modes of thinking, mapping takes full advantage of the symbolic process.

If we want students to generate words easily, if we want them to organize their essays or stories efficiently, if we want them to write coherently, then mapping is one of the skills we will teach. As a prewriting activity it helps students begin, as a shaping activity it helps them form their ideas, as a holistic activity it helps them to synthesize ideas. Because mapping takes advantage of our verbal and visual abilities, it adds a new dimension and power to all language activities, especially writing.

Owen Boyle, Assistant Director, Bay Area Writing Project

MY LIFE, BY LADY MACBETH

After my junior-level English class had read Shakespeare's haunting tragedy, *Macbeth,* most of the students were ready for a break. Instead of a test and as an extension activity, they wrote an autobiography of either Macbeth or his wife, and they chose the tone of their piece—humorous, wistful, thoughtful, or serious. The life story had to span the years from childhood to Act I of the play, and the juncture of the autobiography and the play had to be seamless.

The young authors were asked to invent relationships and events which could logically produce the distinct personalities of the two Macbeths. This creative, right-brained activity appealed to students of all categories. Because students have a fund of observations of various relationships to draw on, they felt confident as they wrote.

The students entered the minds and hearts of their adopted "selves" and demonstrated a mature understanding of cause and effect between events, interpretations of those events, and resulting personalities. Often thoughtful or wistful, the transitions from the characters' happier pasts to their Act I circumstances usually contained a look back to a time of innocence. A few papers included bits of regret, mad courage, or personality quirks from a toxic family environment.

As the students focused on their characters, they confidently went through the process of writing. The initial activity was large-group brainstorming for lists of personality characteristics of Lord and Lady Macbeth, gleaned from the play. After brainstorming, we all talked together about possible goals and experiences of aristocratic, medieval children, and teenagers. Then we came up with some questions for students to use in a make-believe interview with their character, to help stimulate creative thinking: What kind of family did you grow up in? How did you and your parents get along? What responsibilities did you have growing up? What kind of schooling did you have? What were the latest fads when you were a teenager? What concerned you the most at that time? What is your most vivid memory from the past?

We also discussed how to begin the paper, including samples like "Once upon a time . . ." and "My unusual parents spent extra time with all of their children, especially concerning . . . ." Students experimented with possible endings which would blend effortlessly with the time interval, location, and personal development of the character in Act I. For example, a transition sentence for Lady Macbeth might begin, "I have just received a message from my husband at the battlefront. He and his entourage will be here for supper . . . ."

Students continued their prewriting in small groups. I encouraged them to take their notes home over the weekend for additional work which they could then share on Monday in their groups for peer review.

The time frame was usually one day (Friday) for prewriting, including our large-group brainstorming, followed by three days of drafting, revising, and editing (Monday-Wednesday). The students exchanged papers with others in their groups and checked for the following: first, logical events which could produce the husband and wife we met in Act I; second, smooth transitions from their papers to the play; and third, changing the many varieties of *to be* to more dynamic action verbs. Thursday and Friday were set aside for the authors to read their works to the class.

Good writing depends on self-confidence. In their small groups, the young writers talked about the text, the characters, and their ideas for background experiences—learning that they had knowledge and expressive abilities enough to interest their peers. The assignment caused the students to return to the text for specific examples of behaviors and emotions. They were carefully and critically rereading the text for their own purposes now. As they read, they learned to discard superfluous material and to use only the material which fitted their requirements. Concerns about spelling and grammar belonged in the final stages of writing, after the students were satisfied with their content.

Coming before their classmates to read their autobiographies motivated students to do their best, even though classmates were limited to responding with only positive comments following each reading—for instance, "What I like best was . . ." or "You certainly . . . well." I offered suggestions for improvement in private.

Recognizing areas in their pieces which do not work well and getting positive feedback on the effective parts become important lessons for growth. Building self-esteem reduces vulnerability, and self-confidence often engenders a willingness to risk growing and developing as a writer—a worthy goal.

Patricia Gunderlach, Alief Elsik High School, Alief, Texas

THE MANTLE
OF THE EXPERT

My favorite writing assignment on *Macbeth* follows from the belief that students write better when they can write from a position of authority—not a false authority, such as pretending to be literary critics, but an authority based at least partially on their own experiences and their conviction that they can say something significant about a particular topic. Acquiring this authority is particularly difficult for students writing about Shakespeare, who often find themselves defeated by the text and driven to Cliffs Notes or rehashes of class discussion. What these students need is to become comfortable enough with Shakespeare to take a fairly independent look at the plays. Then they can assume what drama educator Dorothy Heathcote calls "the mantle of the expert"—the authority to create.

By the time we get to the paper assignment I describe below, my senior English class has had some experience with Shakespeare. They have read *Hamlet*, seen a videotape of the play, and seen a film illustrating different interpretations of the character of Hamlet. They have discussed characterization and theme and have performed soliloquies. They have also written short personal response papers on the play. After students read *Macbeth* and see a filmed version of the play, they dramatize selected scenes. When they get up on their feet, they are, in a sense, moving from an attempt to get inside the play to projecting the play outside themselves. As they take roles, imagine a stage, search for the tension of a scene, they begin to see a relationship between the parts and the whole. At this point, they are ready to explore the play with even more independence, through the following writing assignment.

I explain to students that they will be writing on "How I Would Direct Act _____ , Scene _____ of *Macbeth.*" Students make their own choices of act and scene. In their papers, students consider and respond to the following questions:

1. What do I think is the function or purpose of this scene in terms of the play as a whole?
2. How would I set the stage? What props would I use to convey my understanding of the scene?
3. What costumes would I use? What type of lighting? What type of music? How would each of these add to the scene?
4. What instructions would I give the actors on how to interpret their roles? What kinds of encouragements would I give to help the actors see this scene the way I see it?
5. What is the overall effect of this scene? What is the effect of my direction? How is my version of this scene different from versions I have seen enacted?

I give students a day or two to think about the questions and to jot down their thoughts, a day to confer with their classmates, and another two days to write up their final versions.

Students enjoy this assignment and invariably do a good job on it. Because of the indirect preparation they have done, the specifics seem to come easily. In fact, some of the resulting papers are almost too imaginative—showing the influences of horror movies and rock videos. But most importantly, the writing shows real involvement on the part of the students. What they put together is their own, and their "expertise" results in better writing.

Sue Howell, Carbondale, Illinois

JOT-LIST POETRY

Writing is fairly easy for students; but when I begin, I usually don't tell them that they're going to write a poem because some students freeze up and say they can't write a poem.

The topics may be on any subject. I've been successful with this activity following a poem called "Childhood Is the Kingdom Where Nobody Dies" by Edna St. Vincent Millay. Students like to think about being kids and have fun recalling details. If you choose childhood as a topic, it isn't necessary to read the Millay poem. These are the steps I use:

1. Conduct a brainstorming session in which students recall details from their childhood, for example, Hot Wheels, Barbie dolls, monsters under the bed, playing soldier, etc. Write all the items on the board under the heading "Childhood is the kingdom where . . . ." However, you may choose another similar prompt: "Summer is the time when . . ." "Elementary school is the place where . . ." etc. Experiment. The board should be fairly well-covered by the end of the brainstorming session.

2. At the top of your paper, write "Childhood is the kingdom where . . . ." Think hard about your topic. What concrete details come to mind? What sensory details—sight, sound, touch, taste, smell—come to mind? What can you see inside your head?

3. Jot down the details as they come to you. Don't stop to evaluate anything at this point. Just write as fast as you can. The longer your jot list, the better.

4. Now read your jot list to yourself. What are the strongest items on your list? Mark them. What are the weakest parts? Can you revise them or should you mark them out?

5. Look again at the items on your jot list. Arrange the items in some kind of logical order. Are there details you need to add? Are there overlapping items? Mark out items that aren't needed. Rewrite your list.

6. Now you will begin to make a poem from your jot list. Begin with "Childhood is the kingdom where . . . ." Repeating that element in the poem could help to unify your piece. Remember, poetry does not

have to rhyme. Reread your jot list carefully. Look for deadweight. Mark out nonessential words. Look for freeloaders like prepositions, conjunctions, or other words not necessary to convey meaning. Read your list aloud to yourself. Can you omit anything without hindering meaning? Do you need to add anything to make parts stronger?

7. Read your list aloud to yourself. Think about cutting out words. Experiment with the order of your ideas. Have you used complete sentences when you don't need them? Where do you need more work?

8. Read your list aloud to yourself. Experiment with line division. Experiment with punctuation. Experiment with stanza form. (Dividing lines to make the poem is more difficult for some students. At this point, I conduct walking conferences to offer suggestions to students who are having problems. There are usually some students who are quite adept at this activity and finish steps while others are still working. Let those students help you work with other students. Some students can provide helpful advice with line divisions and punctuation.)

9. Make another draft of your poem. Read it aloud to yourself. You might share it with a consultant and talk about your poem. Look at it carefully to see if every word carries its weight.

10. When you feel good about your poem, make a final draft.

When I use this activity, I write along with my students and create my own poem. I share with them each step in the process and talk about what I've done, where I've had trouble, what I like, and what I don't like. Students can make some good suggestions. Before I used this activity the first time, I did it on my own to get a feel for it. It's okay to have parts of yours done ahead of time.

I think it's important that the teacher work along with the students. Better yet, asking students for help makes them feel good, and they are more willing to do the activity. If you can get these poems typed, they make a good class publication.

Ed Youngblood, University of Georgia, Athens

Step by Step
TOWARD FEAR-LESS POETRY

Announcement of a poetry unit to my students in the past caused groans and moans, so I was determined to create an assignment that would create positive feelings about poetry. I have successfully used the following assignments for the past two years with English Honors classes.

Step 1

Ask the class to formulate a list of "universal concepts"—things that most people in different parts of the world think are important, care about, fear, wish for, experience, and so on. Some examples are: love, freedom, death, tolerance, prejudice, home, family, suicide, and responsibility. After students discuss and react to the concepts, ask them to write a personal essay expressing their feelings about one of the concepts.

Step 2

Using the main idea or ideas from the paper, each student finds a published poem with the same, similar, or opposing idea or ideas. (As an added benefit of this activity, students may read and enjoy many poems during their search in the library.)

Step 3

Ask each student to create an original poem using the main idea or ideas from his or her essay. Before students begin writing, you may want to talk briefly about the importance of using concrete details and images to create a vivid poem. To the student who needs more guidance, you may give the following suggestions.

    a.   Summarize your essay in one paragraph.
    b.   Use a colored pen to highlight the key words in the paragraph.
    c.   With the key words, arrange a free verse poem. Add other words or phrases if you need to.

Step 4

Sit in a circle and ask each student to read his or her essay, published poem, and original poem. Encourage students to explain how their published poem relates to their essay.

Step 5

Collect original poems and essays from students to make a class anthology. Let students design the cover and add individual touches to the anthology.

This step-by-step approach provides a natural transition into poetry; moving from personal essays to poems, students come to see poetry as another way of expressing thoughts, beliefs, and feelings.

Judy Sunday, Westfield High School, Spring, Texas

POEMS THAT RECREATE THE PAST

If our ancestors could speak to us, what would they say? What advice would they give us? What would they remember most? Would they be sorry about leaving this world, or glad to be finally in the next?

These questions and the poems in Edgar Lee Masters's *Spoon River Anthology* became the basis for a class anthology based on the lives of students' ancestors. Interviewing relatives, writing, and delving into family histories was not a morbid assignment, but a lively one. Most of the students had previously completed either a coat of arms or a family tree, but few had actually investigated the life of a family member.

In the first stage of the assignment, students read selections from Masters's *Spoon River Anthology* and participate in class discussions. In choosing the poems that you want students to read, select several that have young people as subjects.

Students then choose ancestors and research their lives with special emphasis on the eccentricities and characteristics that made them unique.

Student research may involve interviews with family members, looking through family albums, etc. Encourage students to find and bring in photographs of the relatives about whom they are writing.

After completing a fifteen-minute freewriting in class on their ancestors, students read what they have written and list important facts or phrases from the writing that they particularly like. These are then developed into poems. I asked students to work on the poems at home, but they had the opportunity to share their drafts and get feedback in reading/writing groups.

My students became involved with the assignment, and their enthusiasm involved others. One student confessed feeling uneasy writing about his "Pop-Pop" and would not show the poem to his mother because he felt almost "sacrilegious" writing about his grandfather. Perhaps his honesty made him uneasy; nonetheless, his poem is among the best of the collection. Another student chose not to have her poem included in the class anthology. Her poem—a beautifully honest poem about sibling rivalry—showed how she, the younger sister, felt she could not match the accomplishments of her older sister.

The students' poems were sensitive and poignant, and they captured the spirit of the times in which their ancestors lived. The following example especially demonstrates this:

Signora Gabriella

With my husband, I sailed
To a new life in a new country.
A different life in a strange place.
We did not speak the language.
The people viewed us as intruders
And the city was loud and frightening.
But with time came familiarity
And I made the city my home
And it, in its turn, gave me acceptance.
I raised my children and grew old
And watched the silver threads
Replace the black ones in my hair.
Sunny Naples became a bright memory
To think of in the cold winters
When there was no coal for the stove.

In the second stage of the assignment, students try to write about themselves, imagining that they died at their present ages. What would they say from the grave? What have they done to make their families or themselves proud? What were their goals?

The process is the same: freewriting, listing images and phrases, writing the poem, sharing with reading/writing groups, revising, and completing the poem. This part of the assignment was more difficult for my students than writing about their ancestors—most likely because the self-evaluation made them uncomfortable. One notable difference between the two poems was the quality of sadness evident in the poems that students wrote about themselves. Many regretted letting their youths pass without taking time to enjoy life.

When all the poems are completed and typed, set about assembling your own anthology, complete with pictures if possible. Students design a cover, reproduce the contents and cover, and bind the booklets. (We used a GBC binding machine, but you could use a three-hole punch and keep the manuscripts in three-ring binders.)

At the end of the assignment, students have studied American literature, completed original research, participated in the writing process, and published a booklet. Even more important than this, though, is how the students learn to see literature, their ancestry, and themselves from a different point of view by standing in the present and looking back.

Kristen P. Leedom, Alexandria, Virginia

A MODEL ASSIGNMENT

Writing from models can be a very successful writing activity for senior high school students, especially when they can combine use of models with expressions of personal feelings and insights.

Students enjoy adapting their ideas to the demands of the concept, format, and style of an established writer. And the teacher can enjoy using models as a way of examining many aspects of poetry, including theme, language, form, imagery, rhyme, rhythm, and meter.

One particularly successful poem to use as a model is Elizabeth Coatsworth's "Swift Things Are Beautiful."

Swift Things Are Beautiful

Swift things are beautiful:
Swallows and deer,
And lightning that falls
Bright-veined and clear,
Rivers and meteors,
Wind in the wheat,
The strong-withered horse,
The runner's sure feet.

And slow things are beautiful:
The closing of day,
The pause of the wave
That curves downward to spray,
The ember that crumbles,
The opening flower,
And the ox that moves on
In the quiet of power.

After we read the poem together, we talk about its content and form. I like to point out the contrast between the two stanzas and let students examine and compare specific images between the two; then we look more closely at line length, rhyme, and rhythm, and how they are used in each stanza.

To prepare students for writing, I ask them to brainstorm lists of antonym pairs, such as "small and big," "complex and simple," and "summer and winter," as possible subjects. Students share and discuss their lists with one or two other students. Next, they select several pairs from their lists and begin assembling specific details that fit into the categories they have chosen. For instance, the student who elected to contrast "small and big" things chose ladybugs, bees, a mockingbird, diamonds, snowflakes, seashells, and lights on a tree to convey a sense of smallness. The details she chose to represent big things were our planet, the ocean, the moon, the sky, and buildings.

Once students feel they have sufficient details, they reexamine Coatsworth's poem and decide how closely they want to follow her structure and rhyme scheme. They may use free verse if they wish.

Finally, students write their first drafts. After sharing and revising with partners, they complete a final copy for publishing in a book of class poetry.

Patricia Ellis, Huntington Park High School, Huntington Park, California

INCORPORATING THE FINE ARTS

Being a lover of fine art, I have often wondered how I could inspire that same love in my students—seniors in advanced composition and creative writing classes. My inclination was to suppose that since teenagers were more interested in the pop culture they would "turn off" to any use of the fine arts in the classroom. Yet, I still wanted to believe that art could inspire us all. I have experimented with the visual arts as impetus for writing and have found the results *most* satisfying. New to me this year was an advanced composition class of honors students who were obviously good writers. Yet, when I introduced the contrast/comparison paper, I sensed a reticence on their part (and a need for variety on mine). I selected two sets of art prints from the library, being careful to make the contrast in each set obvious. (In this case I paired Modigliani's *Maid* with Chagall's *I and the Village* and Stella's *The Brooklyn Bridge* with Tobey's *Broadway, 1936*.)

Posting the prints on the board at the front of the room, one pair in each corner, I asked my students to select one pair and spend some time just studying what they saw. Then I asked them to write journal entries which focused on finding both similarities (comparisons) and differences (contrasts) within the pictures in the set they had selected. I wondered if students would notice theme, texture, color, movement, or other elements, but not knowing how much experience they had in appreciating art, I didn't know what to expect. Wonderfully, they were both observant and astute in their evaluations and in their abilities to make comparisons and contrasts. They commented on the fact that having something *visually* in front of them increased their ability to notice similarities and differences—an obvious, but often neglected, concept! In fact, students spent far more time in writing, observing, and sharing than I had anticipated. This exercise prepared them to make the transition to an object/idea/situation in a contrast/comparison paper.

A similar experiment proves highly successful in the creative writing class. In this case, as an early poetry assignment, I take my class on an imaginary art field trip by bringing a stack of art prints to the classroom. Then, without commenting on what's ahead, I simply ask students to sit back and enjoy the art show as I hold up each print and make a few simple comments about it. I then place it on display while I show the next print.

After we have viewed all prints, I ask the students to move about the room, viewing the prints again and finally selecting a piece which they could spend some time with.

To my amazement, there are *no* turn-offs. Instead, I find that the interest level is high, and there are often some favorites. It's fine if several students choose the same piece. I then ask students to write a "poem" which centers upon the movement, story line, texture, mood, or color of their selected piece. They are free to change to another print if they now feel unsure of their selection.

Again, the results have always surprised me. Students enjoy the experience, are serious about their endeavors, and create some of their best writing during this assignment. We share these exceptional works with the entire class.

Here is a suggested list of art prints which I have found effective with this activity:

Stella's *The Brooklyn Bridge*
Duchamp's *Nude Descending a Staircase, No. 2*
Tobey's *Broadway, 1936*
Shahn's *Still Music*
Vermeer's *The Little Street*
Davis's *I Saw the Figure Five in Gold (1928)*
Dali's *The Crucifixion*
Chagall's *I and the Village*
Homer's *Breezing Up*
Hopper's *Seven A.M.*
Miro's *Composition 1963*
Wyeth's *Christina's World*
Modigliani's *Maid*

Jean Whiteman, Glenbard West High School, Glen Ellyn, Illinois

Associating the Sister Arts

CREATIVE WRITING, MUSIC, AND PAINTING

The teacher's lounge is not where I ordinarily go to develop new teaching strategies, but in this case, that is just what happened. During lunch in the lounge, one of my colleagues (an arts and humanities teacher) and I (a writing teacher) started discussing the commonalities of our fields. We wondered if we could use these connections to help high school students improve the quality of their writing, especially the writing of short stories.

With the thought of trying out our ideas, we submitted a proposal to the Arkansas Teacher Recognition Program, which awards grants to promising teacher projects. We were fortunate enough to receive a grant, enabling us to design and teach a six-week unit in short story writing, incorporating the visual arts and music as stimuli and resource material. With the grant money, we purchased art supplies, cassette tapes of music, art reproductions, and other instructional materials. In choosing art reproductions, we chose subjects that included landscapes, portraits, genre paintings, and narrative paintings. Few were abstract; most were expressionist or realistic. We took care to select paintings that presented a wide variety of ethnic and cultural subjects. Criteria for selection included the ability of the painting to evoke emotion and stir the imagination and interest of the students. Music selections were based on the same criteria, as well as on the relationship of the musical piece to elements in art and literature, such as mood, theme, and perspective. (No popular or rock music was used.)

Our teaching sequence was a bit unusual. Instead of having students write short stories toward the end of the unit, we started students writing the first day. When they entered the classroom, they were asked to view a selection of paintings, which on that day included Picasso's *The Tragedy*, Wyeth's *Mrs. Kuerner* and *Chambered Nautilus*, and Gauguin's *The Poor Fisherman*. Students were to choose one that interested them and, with that day's musical selection (a piece by Rachmaninoff) playing in the background, were to begin writing a short story using the painting and the music as inspiration. Students began writing without any discussion of mechanics or "correct" writing procedure, and yet the resulting stories contained a great deal of detail and depth. Students' high level of interest continued as they shared their work in small groups.

My colleague and I repeated this same procedure throughout the unit, using paintings and music of varying moods. Each new grouping of paintings and musical selections prompted different observations from students: likes and dislikes, comparisons, comments on style and mood, and thoughts on the parallels or contrasts between the music and the paintings. Gradually students built a whole repertoire of short story beginnings, each with an atmosphere inspired by a different art work and different music.

At one point, we interrupted the writing activities and conducted a series of art lessons in which students drew portraits and abstract works using pastels and chalks. When we returned to writing, the effects of these lessons appeared to carry over: students seemed more concerned with subtleties; their character descriptions were more detailed; and many students began experimenting with using colors to develop mood in their written descriptions, just as they had experimented with color in their drawings. Prompted by a lesson on *line* in art and *tempo* in music, students also practiced varying sentence length according to the tone of the piece of writing.

Finally, we asked students to choose one of their story beginnings and develop it into a complete story. The finished writings, when shared with the class, far exceeded the expectations my colleague and I had had for our unit. In addition, seeing the common themes among works of art, music, and writing increased students' ability to respond to and appreciate works in all of these areas.

For reference, here is a list of some of the art reproductions, music selections, and resources we found useful in teaching this unit:

Art Reproductions
>*The Tragedy*, Picasso
>*The Poor Fisherman*, Gauguin
>*Chambered Nautilus*, Wyeth
>*After School*, Stevenson
>*Mrs. Kuerner*, Wyeth
>*Christina's World*, Wyeth
>*Harmony in Red*, Matisse
>*The Nooning*, Homer
>*Banjo Lesson*, Tanner
>*Boy with Tire*, Lee-Smith
>*Notch of the White Mountain*, Cole
>*Woman with Fan*, Modigliani

View of Toledo, El Greco
Girl with Her Duena, Murillo
The Cafe, Foujita
The Sunny Side of the Street, Evergood
Marriage du Minuit, Magritte
Self-portraits by Van Gogh, Rembrandt, and Beckmann

Music

Rachmaninoff—Concerto No. 2 in C Minor for Piano and Orchestra, Movement II, Adagio sostenuto

Vocalise, Op. 34, No. 14

18th Variation from Rhapsody on a Theme of Paganini

Grieg—Two Elegaic Melodies, Op. 34: "Heart Wounds"

Copland—*Fanfare for the Common Man, Appalachian Spring*

"Hoe-Down" from *Rodeo*

Respighi—*Pines of Rome*

Mussorgsky—*Pictures at an Exhibition*

Resources

Writing Creatively (Amsco School Publications)

Writing Incredibly Short Plays, Poems, Stories by Norton Gretton

A Student's Guide to Creative Writing, by Naomi Long Madgett (Lotus, 1980)

"The Whistle," "Old Mr. Marblehall," and "The Purple Hat," by Eudora Welty (reprinted from her volume *A Curtain of Green and Other Stories* by permission of Harcourt Brace Jovanovich, Inc.)

Brenda Ball and Mary Ann Stafford, Pine Bluff High School, Arkansas

MAKING VIDEOS USER FRIENDLY

English teachers often struggle with the appropriateness of showing videos in class. Since our students love watching them, it can seem as though we're just giving them "free" days. Or are we really showing a video so we can catch up on our own work?

Is there any legitimate reason for showing a video to students? Yes, when it is used as a springboard for writing. Let's face it—our students are visual learners as a result of the video-oriented society we live in. Instead of fighting against the medium, we can use it to our advantage by helping students make connections between reading, viewing, and writing.

A short-story unit provides excellent opportunities for making such connections. (Naturally, it's important that the video be a high-quality, entertaining one chosen at the right level for students.) One assignment that has been successful for me links the short story "Boys and Girls," by Alice Munro, the film *The Man from Snowy River*, and students' personal experiences. It works so well that students write some of their best work of the year. And even if students have seen the movie before, they enjoy watching it together in class.

Before we read the short story, we brainstorm about the title. The students' responses are usually unanimous—boys and girls are different. We discuss many of the societal stereotypes in America, and sometimes other cultures come up as well. We also review the element of theme in short stories. I ask students to keep all this in mind as we read. After reading and discussing the story, we list a few possible themes on the overhead and save these.

We spend the next two class periods watching the video, and students look for comparisons of theme between the two stories. One year, a student remarked, "Man, her father treats her just like the girl's dad in the story we read." I was very pleased as this student went on to make insightful connections between the two stories and our discussion of stereotyping.

Once the video is over, it's time to write. In *Clearing the Way: Working with Teenage Writers* (Heinemann, 1987), Tom Romano suggests doing a quickwrite after the video and before any class discussion so that students can express their thoughts on paper and not be influenced by what other students say. I use the quickwrite as the catalyst for the next brainstorming session for possible themes. The themes generated for this particular assignment tend to deal with stereotypes and young people struggling for independence, topics tenth-grade students relate to well. Other prewriting techniques—webbing, dialoguing with a text, using a pentad—could also be used in addition to or in place of quickwriting.

Once the class compiles a list of five or six possible themes connected to both the short story and the video, each student chooses one or two themes to write about. I explain that students need to take into account that they will be making a personal association to the theme and should choose accordingly.

Now the writing phase begins. Students know they need to refer both to the movie and short story. They know they need to compare the theme to both works and refer to specific examples to support the thesis. They also need to make a personal association to the chosen theme. While students are writing, I confer with students and offer support as needed. I assemble related short stories and novels on a side table for students who finish writing early. Some students may even find another story related to the same theme that they want to incorporate into their final writings.

When students are ready, they meet in peer groups and revise their writing for content and mechanics. Students need to find out if their message is clear to their peer audience. A clocking technique, where students trade papers three or four times and look for specific errors each time, helps students learn in a cooperative atmosphere and helps them polish their final products.

When this activity is completed, students have worked together to produce writings that reflect the connections they made among the video, the short story, and their own lives. This same strategy could be adapted to any genre of literature and could be an effective way to reach all levels of students and all learning styles.

Melinda Mack, Bryan High School, Bryan, Texas

HE SAID, SHE SAID, WE SAID

For an entertaining and effective lesson on persuasive writing and speaking, I've used a little help from Paramount Pictures. In the opening scene of the movie *He Said, She Said,* actors Kevin Bacon and Elizabeth Perkins are debating the merits of "Proposition 41," which proposes a highway merger. Perkins is in favor of the proposition; however, Bacon disagrees with the proposal and supports the status quo. Their opinions are well supported with facts, which my eighth-grade students were quick to discern. I asked my students to watch and listen carefully the first time. After the initial viewing, we discussed what they recalled from the debate. When I played the excerpt a second time, female students are required to note all supporting information that Bacon presents. Male students, on the other hand, are required to record all of Perkins's supporting information.

Often, the dialogue that follows their observations is quite interesting, and brainstorming about a variety of "local" topics occurs naturally, inspiring a variety of interesting possibilities for writing.

After students have listed their own topics of interest, they select one to write about. They may next do some further research on their topics by reading local newspaper editorials. One newspaper my students drew on, for example, provided the opposing views on corporal punishment in the schools. Another editorial presented different views on censorship by school principals. Students enjoy discussing issues that are directly related to their interests, of course, so using these topics resulted in active learning, participation, and productivity.

Ultimately, the students compose their own editorials via the writing process. After developing polished drafts, students prepare to deliver their editorials in front of the class. We videotape the editorials and air them in our weekly class "news broadcast." Students really enjoy viewing and critiquing their editorials. They like emulating the stars in the movie; in fact, they often draw some interesting comparisons to the excerpt. Most importantly, students appreciate the amount of time, effort, creativity, and skill necessary to compose and produce an effective editorial.

Note: I purchased the videotape of *He Said, She Said* at a low price, and have seen it advertised at a similar price in a video catalog. The film is relevant for other units of study as well. For example, I've also used it for symbolic and metaphoric analysis, since the proposal of the highway merger really represents a marriage proposal.

Sherry Clark, Peters Township Middle School, McMurray, Pennsylvania

THE STORY-CONSTRUCTS PROCESS

Many independent writing periods have been interrupted by cries of "How long does it have to be?" or "I can't think of anything to write." For the price of a newspaper, you can silence these cries and lead students to some healthy realizations about writing. The newspaper is your source for a set of "story constructs"—frameworks around which students will ultimately develop prose pieces or expository essays.

In providing a framework of characters and events, story constructs offer students a useful jumping-off point for developing their storywriting talents and for observing the decisions they make as they write. Students are freed from questions of who and what, allowing them to focus on more subtle elements of the writing process, and to evaluate more objectively their choices in regard to organization, use of detail, dramatic possibilities for the characters and events, and other issues that come up during the creation of a story.

The first step is to select from a daily newspaper or a student news publication one article to use as a focus. This should not be a world-news headline story but rather an open-ended human interest feature which you feel will catch your students' interest. Among the topics of stories I've used are Etan Patz, the missing child; David, the "bubble boy"; David Rothenberg, the "burn boy"; and the mysterious death of Swale, the champion racehorse. The Wallace series of book lists also includes various actual unsolved cases which you might want to use as story constructs.

Since you and your students will be spending at least three class sessions and much thought on each construct, consider the emotional effect of heavy concentration on a particular construct. Decide whether you want your students to dwell on situations which could involve violent solutions. Your decision will be governed by the grade and maturity levels of your students. You may choose to focus on stories dealing with animals or with positive family values.

Introduce your selected newspaper story by discussing it with the students before they receive their own copies. In the case of the "Etan Patz, missing child" construct, I asked students, "Did you ever get lost when you were five or six? How did you feel?" "How did you find your parents, or how were you returned to your parents?" Preliminary class discussion may take fifteen minutes. Then give each student a copy of the article. In addition, you may opt to project the whole article or its opening paragraph on the overhead for the students to consider as a group.

Students should be given five to ten minutes to read the article. They should have pen and paper in hand and should jot down the following items: characters (the names of the characters involved in the news story and important or intriguing details about them), setting (a description of the story's location), the basic situation or events of the story, and any direct quotes made by the characters. In the Etan Patz case, for example, the personalities included Etan, age 6; Stan, his father; Julie, his mother; his older sister; and various neighbors. The situation section detailed the specific circumstances involving Etan's walking from his home to the bus stop for the first time and the reports that he never boarded the bus.

Finally, after the students have shared and enlarged their outlines of characters, quotes, setting, and situation, invite them to explore the "dramatic possibilities." Explain that you are asking them as writers and as involved readers to expand on the original facts of the story, to "guess" or speculate on certain aspects of the story or on what happens next. Dramatic possibilities might include the following: the ending or sequel set five years later; a prequel to the story, telling what happened before the story began; the story as told from the viewpoint of one of the major or minor characters; imagined dialogue or conversation between characters involved in the story; an interior monologue in stream-of-consciousness style by one of the characters; a poem or short story based on the news story; or a news story on the significance of the events in relation to other news.

In the Etan Patz case, for example, my students speculated on the moment of Etan's actual disappearance, on where Etan was at the very moment they were writing about him, on Etan's sister's view of what happened and how it affected her life, on a conversation between Etan's parents, and on the significance of the Patz case as an incentive for fingerprinting and missing child legislation.

The entire first period of the story-constructs process is devoted to talk and sharing of student reaction to the construct. The only writing done is the jotting down of details regarding characters, quotes, setting, and situation. *No formal writing of the composition takes place during this period.* This is done purposely to involve the students in the nuances of the case. Students' assignment for the next session will be to develop any one of the story-constructs possibilities.

The second session of the story-constructs technique opens with a most pleasing lack of the usual "but I didn't know what to write about" complaints. Every student will have worked from a detailed outline featuring characters, situation, setting, quotes, and a lengthy list of dramatic possibilities. Even the students who did not actively participate in the discussion had the benefit of listening to others toss around various viewpoints and possibilities. To begin the second session, ask for three volunteers from the class who wish to share their work. If your students are shy, you might pick out three of the papers to read aloud, without mentioning the authors' names, or you might suggest that a shy writer have another student function as a "reader" for his or her work. Everyone in class is given a "Story-Construct Suggestion Sheet," which asks for the following information:

Story Construct No. 1 (Title)_____.
The dramatic possibility used was _____.
The good points of this construct were _____.
The author should work on _____.
I would suggest that the author _____.
Overall, I really liked _____ about
    this story construct.

The same information is requested for the other two story constructs to be read. The student evaluation sheet deliberately begins and ends with the positive aspects of the presentation.

For the reading, the author or chosen reader of story construct No. 1 takes center stage. The story is read. Make no comments during this session except for positive closing remarks after all the students have spoken. The author or his or her reader asks, "What were the good points about the story?" (Students offer their responses.) "In what ways might the story be improved?" (Again, each student's response is heard.) "What did you really like about this story?"

Most teachers who use this technique are surprised by the objectivity and degree of detail with which students respond to this student-controlled self-critiquing session. The critiquing session has some built-in safeguards against failure. The student who volunteers to read or have his or her work read usually has something to be proud of. Students enjoy the idea of controlling the session. Peer or immediate audience feedback, especially when it is positive, is a powerful motivator and a rich reward for writing.

The teacher checks the students' progress during this session, but the papers are not yet collected to be graded. The students are given another week to revise their initial first drafts. Although only three papers are discussed during the second session, the discussion and peer feedback are invaluable writing incentives for all students. Papers turned in at the third session are generally detailed and well developed.

The story-constructs process can be implemented in grades four through high school. Besides enhancing critical reading and expository writing skills, this activity trains students to extract characters, details, and situations which can function as building blocks for their own literary creations. It promotes student involvement in current affairs and sensitizes students to the concern of others. Once you begin this process with your students, you'll have a captivated and motivated classroom of writing aficionados.

Rose Reissman, Bay Terrace School, Bayside, New York

3 | EMPHASIS: PEER EDITING, SELF EDITING, REVISION

CONSTRUCTIVE FEEDBACK

Writers have many ways to get feedback about their work while revising. But many student writers and peer editors focus primarily on "fixing up" a text, getting rid of surface errors in spelling and punctuation. Thus writers are often unaware that even readers who praise their text may be missing their point. The following activity helps students provide accurate, constructive feedback.

Students work in pairs, taking turns as reader and writer. The reader reads the writer's paper aloud, pausing periodically to answer aloud the following questions:

First part of paper:
> Begin reading the paper. After each sentence, ask yourself, Is this the point the author will be talking about? If no, continue reading. If yes, do the following: Restate the main point in your own words. Predict what you think will come next in the paper.

Periodically:
> What is the point of this section? How does it fit with the paper so far? What do you predict is coming next?

End of paper:
> Summarize the main point and the main parts of the paper. Is there anything confusing in the paper? Is there anything with which you disagree or which makes you want additional information? What is best about the paper?

As the reader answers these questions, the author listens and takes notes, with comment or oral explanation.

At the end of the reading, writers have several kinds of information. They know whether the reader got the main point, including whether the reader had to struggle to find it or whether it was evident and clear. Writers know where the reader expected examples, a definition, or another main point. They hear the paper taking shape and ideas being emphasized or de-emphasized. In sum, writers can make more informed decisions about their text.

A number of variations are possible for this activity:

- Two students might read the paper aloud, thus providing more information to the writer.

- Writers can tape-record a reading. This method works especially well for long or complex texts, where young writers may not be able to remember what they have written, or where writers may be unable to take sufficient notes.

- Readers might read the text on a computer screen, adding their comments or suggestions to the file.

- Using an overhead projector, teachers or writers can project one sentence at a time for class response. Readers who have alternative predictions can be encouraged to explain how they arrived at their predictions. Writers are often surprised at how a text can lead readers to expect unintended moves.

- As an author explains part of a text orally, other students can be invited to offer alternative sentences based on their perspectives on the text.

This activity takes practice. Initially, some students may feel uncomfortable reading aloud. However, using this feedback method in a class with everyone speaking to a partner can reduce the discomfort of hearing just one's own voice. Modeling the method also helps reduce discomfort, as does class discussion.

If students are accustomed to keeping a journal or notes on their writing process, they might include a record of what they heard and how they responded. Over time, they will find themselves making predictions about what readers will say. In effect, they are forming hypotheses about strong and weak parts of the paper. Later, students' journal entries often record their pleasure at being understood and their awareness of learning how to anticipate a reader's needs.

Barbara M. Sitko, Washington State University, Pullman, Washington

SPINNING WHEEL OF WRITING PARTNERS

H ere is an idea I use in conjunction with a series of daily ten-minute writing assignments and occasionally with longer assignments.

I cut a large outer circle and a smaller inner circle out of two different colors of construction paper. I place the smaller circle on top of the larger and draw half as many lines radiating out from the center as there are students in my class. I write the names of half the class (the first half, proceeding alphabetically through my class roster) along the lines in the center circle and the names of the other half along the lines in the outer circle. A brad fastener in the center permits the inner wheel to turn while the outer one, which I attach to the bulletin board, is stationary. Thus, by using the wheel to determine partner pairings for writing assignments, I give students the chance to work with at least half the class. In practicing writing and revising in pairs, students are exposed to different ideas and different writing styles.

Some of the writing assignments I give require that partners actually write something together; others require that the partners write separately, exchange papers to respond to one another's work, and then discuss their responses in class the next day. Listed below are examples of both types of assignments.

Joint Writing Assignments

Together with your partner, plan and write a strategy or outline of steps for how you would solve a particular problem.

Discuss with your partner a novel or story you have both read. Together, plan and write a critical essay about the work.

Writing and Responding Assignments

Imagine that you have just turned thirty. Write about your dreams for the future. Describe also the ways in which your life is different from the expectations you had in high school.

Then exchange papers with your partner and write your responses to such questions as "What parts did you enjoy most?" "What words or phrases stood out?" "What parts would you suggest revising?" Talk with your partner about your responses to his or her writing.

Imagine that you are taking an evening walk outside. Notice your environment closely as you walk and write down everything you perceive with your senses.

After writing, exchange papers with your partner. Write your responses to his or her writing, and share your feedback.

Ily Leavy, Greeley West High School, Colorado

MEMORIES AND MEMENTOS

Almost everyone preserves memories in some way, whether by purchasing souvenirs, pressing flowers in a book, making photo collages, or another means. I take advantage of this fact of human nature in the following assignment, in which I participate along with my students.

First, I make this request of students: "Over the next few days, look through items that you have saved as mementos. Find one in particular that recalls a vivid memory, one which enabled you to comprehend for the first time the meaning of an abstraction such as joy, misery, disappointment, pride, defeat, or some other. This item may be anything from a T-shirt to a theater ticket as long as it can be transported to school."

Next, I explain the writing assignment: "Your task will be to project yourself into the future and give yourself celebrity status. Imagine that a weekly news magazine supplement has asked you to write a short (one- to two-page) memoir in which you recreate a certain moment in your life. In this memoir, you are to describe the moment you came to understand the real meaning of joy, misery, disappointment, or whatever feeling your memento symbolizes for you."

Before students begin writing, I lead some prewriting activities. I read aloud excerpts from autobiographical memoirs (Mark Twain's and Gordon Liddy's are both quite powerful) and from poetry that draws on real life (such as Anne Sexton's "Pain for a Daughter," or Phillip Lopate's "Once a Long Time Ago"). I ask students to talk about the emotions conveyed through these writings, and to suggest concrete items that might trigger the memories described.

In another prewriting activity, students form pairs and exchange mementos. Students then consider what kinds of feelings the object might recall for its owner (pleasant, wistful, nostalgic, and so on). Students ask one another questions, explain their reactions to one another and then return the objects.

Students may also close their eyes and recall all the sense impressions they associate with the object. In each pair, the listening student records the impressions in list form, and then the students switch roles.

When students are ready to begin writing their "memoirs" for the fictional magazine, I give them these suggestions: "Go over the list of sensory details you dictated to your partner and choose those that most closely and accurately recreate the memory for you. Try to work these details into natural images without forcing them. If necessary, look back for inspiration at the language used in the poems we read. You may either begin with your abstraction and illustrate it with specific details, or begin with specifics and lead into your abstraction, building a sense of revelation at the end."

After writing, students reform their pairs. Each student writes detailed responses to these questions for his or her partner:

Does the written draft illustrate the same feelings conveyed by the
    oral version?
Does the introduction indicate the direction of the paper?
Has the writer used details that stir all the senses?
Does the memoir have a strong and appropriate conclusion?

Students have a week from the date of the peer response session to complete a polished draft. Pairs of students may then move into groups of six to read their final drafts aloud.

Janet Glitzenstein, Glastonbury High School, Connecticut

IT'S ALL IN YOUR POINT OF VIEW

News stories and editorials can provide excellent examples of objectivity and of slanted writing. I use such articles in my classroom to help students understand a variety of points of view.

I find that the more controversial the subject of the article, the more detailed the response from my students. One article that generated particular interest in my class was entitled "Turning in Their Parents: Love or Betrayal?" The subject was a thirteen-year-old girl who, after some deliberation and agonizing, turned in her parents to the authorities for drug use.

I gave students three short writing assignments related to this article. In prewriting discussion, I asked students to consider the implications of the headline. We used the chalkboard to list the pros and cons of the girl's decision, and then placed the names of the various authorities in either the pro or con column, depending on the person's views. I asked students to offer possible reasons for the widely conflicting opinions expressed in the article and to judge the level of objectivity of the article. I also asked them how reporters might get around being totally objective. I then distributed a handout sheet containing the following assignments and guidelines for writing.

Assignments

1. Write three diary accounts in the first person from the point of view of the central character—the thirteen-year-old girl. Choose key dates in the girl's life and trace her thoughts to the moment of her decision.

2. For the morning edition of the local paper, write a brief column (three or four paragraphs) from the stance of a reporter who happened to be in the police station when the girl made her statement.

3. Write the response given to a roving TV reporter by the neighbor who drove the girl to the police station and stayed with her during her statement. Use an editorial voice that is deliberately slanted for or against the girl.

Guidelines

For assignment #1: Start with the diary accounts. Remember, you are seeing things through the eyes of a thirteen year old; choose images and language accordingly. Consider physical sensations that would accompany her emotional state and ways in which her view of the world might be distorted. Try to convey a sense of growing panic.

For assignment #2: Write from a reporter's stance. Imagine yourself as a camera's eye and a tape recorder. Use your information to compose an objective column for the morning edition of the newspaper. Remember to cover the five W's—who, what, when, where, and why—in the first paragraph.

For assignment #3: Finally, assume the persona of the neighbor. You witnessed everything the reporter did—but from a biased position. Write out the version you gave to the news reporter. Feel free to use loaded language.

After students have completed all three assignments, I collect the papers and choose three writings at random (one sample from each category) to put on the overhead and to critique in class, with students' help. Students receive a copy of the criteria listed below. I stress that these are the same criteria that I will use in the assessment of final drafts.

1. Do the diary accounts reflect the language and thoughts of a young teen? What specific words or phrases seem out of place?
2. Is there a sense of growing tension?
3. Does the writer consistently maintain a first-person voice, yet without an overload of *I*? What would be some ways to edit *I* from the text?
4. Is the reporter's stance objective throughout? If not, what opinions and loaded words could be revised?
5. Does the neighbor focus on the thirteen-year-old girl or does he or she shift emphasis to himself or herself? If the latter, how could the focus be shifted back to the main character (the girl)?
6. Are we placed in the appropriate sensory world of each of the three speakers?
7. Is the punctuation used correctly, especially where quotations are included in the text?

After our critique of the three samples, students may reevaluate their writings. The revision stage merits workshop time in class. I encourage students with questions to meet with their peers and with me.

Upon completion of this assignment, students seem to have a clearer idea of how point of view can be used in writing and how different points of view affect the selection of details.

Janet Glitzenstein, Glastonbury High School, Connecticut

MODELING TOPIC GENERATION AND PEER EDITING

This approach to topic generating and peer editing has two particular benefits: it increases student writing and lessens the paper load. For this procedure to succeed, you—the teacher—must act as a model, completing each of the steps first and giving students examples to follow. The effectiveness of this process is also dependent on students being able to discuss their writing with one or more other students and on the activity being made as nonthreatening as possible. Your modeling will help somewhat in setting the stage.

Here are guidelines for using this approach in the classroom.

TOPIC GENERATING

Number a paper from one to four. Try to think of four possible writing topics: people you have known, places you have visited, things you have done, and so on. These may be pleasant or unpleasant memories. (The purpose of starting with personal narrative is that the writer already has the information and need not be encumbered by outside sources.) As you model this step, comment briefly on each of the four topics and share a few details about each one with the class. Then ask students to pair off, think of four topics, and relate them briefly to their partners.

Next, take one of your four topics—the one you feel would be easiest to write about—and recall as much about it as possible, thinking aloud for the benefit of your class. Copy down single word cues on the board to remind you of what you have said. Don't worry at this point about ordering or theme development.

Ask for one or two questions from the class about your topic. Then ask students to go through the same process, thinking of topics, jotting down cues, and talking with their partner using the cues. Listeners are to ask one or two questions, but there is to be no other dialogue.

By the time this process is completed, most writers have enough ideas to attempt a first, "free-flow" draft. Make sure students know that their free-flow drafts are personal and that no one else will see them. Students shouldn't yet worry about neatness or proper mechanics.

Time this first draft, allowing students seven to ten minutes to write nonstop. Write a first draft of your own on the topic you selected earlier, and read your draft to the class, pointing out rough edges, unclear language, and other parts you might want to revise. Explain the value of "focusing"—zeroing in on one section or idea that could use more detail. It will help students if you demonstrate this technique by selecting one area of your own draft to focus on.

Students then select portions of their own papers that could benefit from the focus technique. Tell students that this revised draft will be seen only by two or three other students in a peer editing group. Take time to explain the value of having audience reaction throughout the writing process. Then give students seven to ten minutes to write a second draft of their papers.

PEER EDITING

After the second draft is completed, group students in threes and fours. Try to create a mix of abilities and personalities. Assign numbers to students in each group, indicating who reads first, second, third, and so on. Then distribute half-sheets of paper on which two columns are labeled: "good" and "more."

In their groups, students take turns reading their papers aloud. There is to be no discussion, merely careful listening. Each student reads his or her paper twice, reading slowly the second time to give the other group members time to jot down reactions. In the "good" column, students write one-word indications of strong word choices or ideas of interest. Areas of the paper that are confusing or that need attention are indicated by single-word entries in the "more" column. Students should be forewarned that this is not meant to be an in-depth analysis. And, to help the writer as much as possible, group members should try to make entries in both columns. As a preface to this group work, it may be a good idea for you to read your own focus paper to the class and ask students to jot down their reactions in the two-column format.

Using the "good" and "more" notes they have received from their peers, students prepare a "best effort" paper. In this paper, for the first time in the assignment, students are asked to consider organization, proper mechanics, and neatness. Before students return to their groups to circulate these "best effort" papers, you will probably want to coach them on what things to look for in the writing and editing. Then, in their groups, students make corrections and comments as they see the need. Again, discussion is discouraged at this stage.

Using the revised version of their papers, students prepare a final draft, which is submitted for grading. It's a good idea to ask students to write several papers using this procedure. This way, students may each select one of their papers to be assigned a letter grade: the others may be assigned an "effort" grade. Since the objective is for students to practice writing and to benefit from peer review of their writing, you needn't feel obliged to scrutinize every paper. This allows for maximum writing and minimum paper burden. As the peer evaluation process becomes more comfortable for the class, the words "good" and "more" on the review sheets can be replaced with specific critical elements supplied by the teacher. Teaching students how to react to the writing of others will teach them to improve their own.

Dale Fournier, Warren Consolidated Schools, Michigan

STUDENTS TAKE OWNERSHIP OF THEIR REPORTS

How many students have you known who, when faced with an assignment for a report, turn out a collection of copied or barely paraphrased paragraphs from several source books? I believe that this tendency can be reduced, if not prevented, through careful teaching and monitoring of note taking and report writing. To that end, I have developed and implemented a lesson that uses modeling and guided follow-up strategies often ignored in report writing. This assignment can be effective at many levels.

The procedure involves a saturation report, an assignment to which I was introduced at the Summer Institute of the East Asia Writing Project. A saturation report is a human-interest article so named because the reporter saturates himself or herself with the atmosphere of a location before writing about it. The major characteristics of a saturation report are that it appeals to the senses; it re-creates the atmosphere of the place; and it makes use of dialogue or interview material. I have found that this assignment helps students take ownership of their subject and write with more originality.

Each student drafts two saturation reports, taking at least one through the entire writing process. The student writes the first report on a place that we all visit together. Students visit the second location in groups of two or three.

I choose places with a variety of stimuli so that students will have multiple sensory reactions to the place. The school in which I developed this sequence was large enough that I chose sites within the grounds. In other situations, a teacher might prefer to move out into the community.

In preparing for the first visit, I share with the class the criteria for a saturation report, and I read a sample report from a previous class or from a magazine. I hand out a worksheet with one column for each of the five senses, modeling its use as if we were going to write about our classroom. We talk about how in some cases one might have to use a bit of imagination with the senses of taste and smell.

I tell the class our first destination, and we brainstorm a list of people to interview and the questions to ask. I point out that open-ended questions will make the interview more interesting and informative. The high school library and the swimming pool have both worked well as sites for the visit.

For the second report, I try to find enough places to offer students a choice. Students should go to unfamiliar places. Among those I have used are the home economics room, the business education class, the computer lab, the high school gym, a drama class in the theater, the high school band room, an ESOL class, the office, the resource room, the batik area of the art department, and other classrooms. Shy students seem to prefer places closer to their own environment and experience, such as a classroom, but there are more adventurous students who want to go somewhere completely foreign to them.

Each person makes at least two visits to his or her particular site for this second report. Students write the first draft during a class period between the two visits. This allows a chance for other classmates and me to read and respond to their reports with comments and questions and for the author to obtain additional information on the second visit. To elicit concrete remarks, I ask students to respond to the following questions or directives about each saturation report:

- To how many senses did the author appeal? Give quotations to support your answers.
- Did the author use descriptive language effectively to give you a "feel" for the place? Illustrate your answer with quotations.

- Did the author use dialogue or interviews? If yes, was this information effective? If no, whom would you suggest that the author interview?
- Tell the author, in your own words, what you think this place is like, based on his or her report.
- Ask questions of the author. What else would you like to know? Was anything unclear?

After the visits, we spend more class time on revising and editing the reports. Then we put the reports together into a book. We make several copies in order to loan it out to parents, classmates, and people from our visits. Later, when I assign the traditional research report, I feel that it is easier for students to take ownership of the report, evaluating, sorting, and digesting the information that they uncover.

Elizabeth A. Neat, Loren Miller Elementary School, Los Angeles, California

KEEPING STUDENT CRITICS HONEST

I have always believed that peer evaluation is a valuable experience for both the writer and the critic. However, for me, this exercise has always been more successful in theory than in practice. I've often been disappointed with the results, sensing that students were hesitant to be honest in their evaluations because they feared their peers would be offended or angered by their comments. Student critics would write vapid, generic comments that were of little value to the writer. This year, as part of an autobiography unit, I tried something new and was very pleased with the results. Here are the steps I follow for this week-long assignment.

Day 1
I ask students to take five to ten minutes to write down ten events from their childhood. They are then to choose one that they would be willing to share

with the class. (This is an effective way to get students into a narrative mood.)

We then form a circle and begin telling the stories. I always go first to break the ice. This seems to relax students and helps them realize that this is a nonthreatening activity; it's not even graded!

I then choose a student to go next. The student tells the story and chooses someone to go next. This process continues until the end of the hour. We don't usually have time for all students to tell their stories, but the mind-set has been established. (Students sometimes convince me to listen to the rest of the stories the next day.)

Day 2
I hand out and explain to students the evaluation sheet shown below:

1. Does the beginning of the story capture your interest? How? Which words? If not, how could it be improved?
2. What is the focus of the incident? (What is this story about?)
3. What are *three* phrases you especially liked? Explain why you liked them.
4. What is something you wanted to know more about?
5. What are two or three things that are weak or confusing in this incident?
6. Could the events in the narrative be arranged in a more effective order?
7. Where could direct quotations or conversation be used to create a clearer picture of the character's feelings?
8. Talk about the pace of the story. Is there variety? Where does the pace need altering to be more effective?

I point out that we will be using this list to evaluate three stories together in class; eventually students will use the same form to evaluate a piece of writing from a student in one of my other classes.

I choose three pieces of narrative writing, very different in style and quality, each approximately 200 to 400 words long. I hand out copies of the first of these and read it aloud. Students then use the list above to evaluate the writing, jotting their comments and responses on the copy of the story rather than on the evaluation sheet. (We save the sheet until later.) I give students ten minutes for this step before class discussion of our responses. Then I read the next piece of writing and follow the same procedure as was used with the first. Afterwards, we discuss the differences between the two pieces of writing.

Day 3
I continue with a third piece of narrative writing, a piece that is obviously inferior to the first two examples. As before, I ask students to evaluate it, but

then I take the process one step further.

I ask students to rewrite the selection and to make the changes that they suggested based on the evaluation sheet. The last ten minutes of class are spent sharing some of the best parts of these rewrites with the rest of the class. I tell students that the next day they will be taking their childhood memory from Day 1 and turning it into a 200- to 400-word, polished narrative.

Day 4
Students have the entire period to work on their childhood-memory narratives, which are due at the end of the hour.

Day 5
Finally we actually write on the evaluation sheet! I code the compositions from each class with a number that corresponds to the student's name and number in the gradebook. I then cut off the name and distribute the papers to another class, giving each student a composition to evaluate. Now students each write comments on the evaluation sheet.

Students have about twenty minutes to read and criticize the narratives in front of them. I then collect the writings, read over the comments to make sure they are appropriate, give the evaluators points for their comments, cut off their names, and redistribute the papers to the authors the next day. The student critics never know the authors, nor do authors know who evaluated their writings.

This method has been a vast improvement over previous attempts at peer evaluation. I have been amazed at the honesty and earnestness with which students have evaluated their peers' writings. In addition, the revised narratives showed definite improvement. Students had obviously given thought and credence to the comments of their peers.

Jule Adelsheim, Osseo Senior High School, Osseo, Minnesota

| WHY REVISE?

Many inexperienced writers think that the first draft is the finished copy. How can we teachers who teach writing help our students see the importance of second and third drafts?

I hold drafting sessions in which I focus on questions that reinforce the need for further drafts. These questions, which include some of my own and some suggested by students, help students rethink the ideas in their drafts and also give me a chance to touch on specific areas, such as sentence length, sentence structure, and topic development. I use this strategy with college freshmen, but it could be successful at any level.

To each drafting session the student brings two copies of his or her draft— one for me and one for the exchange. I vary the format of the drafting sessions to make them even more effective. For example, for one session I might ask students to pair up and exchange drafts; for another I might ask students to work in "workshops" of four or five students each; for a third session students might meet as a whole class to examine copies of several different drafts and to discuss possible revisions together.

At each session I give students only as many questions as they can respond to fully in the time allotted. Here are some sample questions concerning idea development that I might use in a drafting session:

What is the topic? (Underline the topic each time you see it repeated.)
Did the writer tell the reader anything new?
What will the reader know after reading this?
Who could benefit from this information?
What detailed examples did the writer use?
What, if anything, do you think needs to be added to give a clearer picture of the topic?
What are some of the main ideas that the writer uses to support his or her thesis?
Can you think of any ideas not currently included that the writer might want to add in a revised draft?

Student authors can then refer to the written responses to these questions as they revise their writing.

The revision process is a necessary one for any writer. Once my student writers realize that the first draft is just a preliminary one, I am plagued less often by the question "Why revise?"

Edwina K. Jordan, Illinois Central College, East Peoria, Illinois

A Writing Teacher's Guide to
PROCESSING SMALL-GROUP WORK

Many teachers have discovered great value in using peer writing groups in the classroom. However, some of us are concerned that students may not gain as much through the group experience as we would like. What teachers often feel they lack is processing (or debriefing) skills—strategies to promote their students' immediate examination of what they have just done in groups.

Most students are not yet capable of both extracting the purpose of their activity from their experience and evaluating their accomplishments. These are sophisticated skills. As professional educators, we can provide the structure within which our students can develop their abilities of self-examination.

In short, this is what a processing session is all about: it should invite students to contemplate what is happening to them as writers and as members of peer writing groups.

What Is Processing?
Processing is a teacher-led activity that immediately follows small-group work. The teacher assumes the role of facilitator, which involves questioning, suggesting, and directing the discussion. It helps if students are seated in a somewhat circular or horseshoe arrangement, individually or clustered in groups. The more eye contact each student can make with others in the entire group, the more likely they all will be to engage in dialogue rather than to speak only to the teacher.

What Should I Do?
As facilitator, you will select two or three key questions to focus the discussion.

You might join your students by taking a chair in the circle. Or you could stand outside the circle, moving about and making eye contact with all. In a horseshoe arrangement, you might sit or stand in the opening. In either arrangement, standing communicates more teacher control over the activity, while sitting turns more of the control over to the students.

Because a major purpose of small-group processing is to encourage students to accept responsibility for their own learning, you can help your students most by working toward less teacher control. Your decisions about that, however, may vary from one class to another, from one age group to another, and even from one moment to the next during a single session. You may find, for instance, that if you stand early in the session, restless students settle down more quickly. Once discussion is under way, your taking a seat may go unnoticed and will not affect student dialogue.

How Long Should a Processing Session Last?

The answer could be two minutes, or twenty, or more—depending on your objectives and your students' ages and attention spans. In some activities you might want students to reassemble as a class for a feeling of closure or togetherness before the school day or class period ends. Working in small groups without even a brief return to the large group can bring feelings of fragmentation or incompleteness to the activity. For a short debriefing with young children, you might simply ask, "How many of you had a good idea today while you wrote? What good idea did you hear in your group that you'd like the entire class to hear?" Then, after one or two students have shared their ideas, that day's session could end.

What Questions Should I Ask?

Your questions will depend on many considerations: how experienced your students are as writers and small-group workers, what type of writing they're doing, what the small group was asked to accomplish, where you are in your instructional plans. The two or three questions you select will focus the ensuing discussions; therefore, you should develop questions that lead to the writing and sharing goals you have in mind. In any case, processing, like all educational experiences, should be approached *developmentally*. Design the processing so that it encourages students to (1) explore their writing and small-group behavior, (2) "own" what they discover about their behavior, and (3) act on these discoveries appropriately.

The following are some questions that you might ask, depending on the developmental goals for your class(es):

To encourage students to gain control over their writing processes:
> Was it easy or difficult to get started? Why?
> Describe the moment you put pen to paper.

What happens to you *physically* while you write?

Do you reread and rewrite? How does that happen for you?

Did the time for writing seem long? Short?

Where does your writing seem to be going?

What do you do about planning throughout the process?

Did any of you make an outline? When? What does it look like?

When can you tell you're finished with a piece?

To encourage students to assume responsibility for their products:

What kinds of writing did you do today?

How much did you get to write in the time you had?

Does your writing today add up to something?

Has your writing arrived somewhere? Where?

Have you made it clear why you wanted to write the piece you're working on?

How can you find out if your piece said what you wanted it to?

What do you want to do with this writing?

To encourage students to consider their environmental needs *for writing:*

What writing tools do you like to use?

How would you describe your writing habits?

What sort of setting do you like for writing?

What can you do to help yourself write in the classroom?

At what time of day or night do you like to write?

How much time does "setting up" take?

To encourage students to acknowledge their attitudes *about writing:*

How did you feel when I asked you to write?

Does anyone feel anxious about getting started?

Can you describe how writing makes you feel?

What is it about writing that sometimes makes you anxious?

Which part of your piece brought you the most pleasure (or pain) as you wrote?

How did you feel when you read your piece?

Where do you think these feelings come from?

Why do many of us make apologies for our pieces before we read them?

How did you feel about the responses your group gave you today?

How does feeling angry (or afraid, happy, etc.) affect your ability to write?

To encourage students to develop small-group working strategies:

What were some of the responses you received in your group today?

What are you doing when members of your group apologize before they read?

How can you include your groupmates who may not talk as much as you?

How do you make sure everyone gets to read?

How much of your group discussion was on track? Off track? Whose responsibility is that?

What do you do when all the members of your group think you need to write something differently?

Evaluation of Processing

How do you evaluate the success or failure of your processing efforts? Through results. If your students gradually show more interest in the process (their own and their peers'), if they assume increasing concern about the products they hand in, if they show courtesy for others while they write, if they talk openly about how writing makes them feel, and, finally, if they work more effectively in their groups as the semester wears on, then there is a very good chance that your processing time is working.

Remember, debriefing your students after small-group work, like writing, is a *process*. You get better at it the more you practice.

E. Kathleen Booher, Old Dominion University, Norfolk, Virginia. Reprinted from Focus on Collaborative Learning *(NCTE, 1988).*

WHO HAS TIME TO READ?

An effective proofreading and editing technique called the "clock" was introduced by Irene Payan in "Peer Proofreading" (*Classroom Practices in Teaching English, 1979-1980: How to Handle the Paper Load*; NCTE, 1979). I learned about this technique from a colleague who attended a writing workshop.

After arranging desks in two concentric circles, half the students sit in the inner circle, facing outward; the rest sit in the outer circle, facing inward. Students begin by exchanging papers with their partners in the other circle. Accompanying each paper is an editing sheet on which students are to write their comments. Starting with the first item on a list prepared by the teacher, students check the papers for one or two specific points. Students note any errors on the editing sheet and return all papers to their owners. Then students in the outer circle move over one desk in a clockwise direction. Papers are again exchanged, and students check the next item on the editing list. This procedure continues until all items have been checked. The exercise ends with students making neat corrections on their papers before handing the assignment in to be graded.

I have found many occasions for using "clocking," but the two most beneficial involved research papers and final exams. When using clocking with research papers, I set aside three days. First, students checked title pages, outlines, bibliographies, pagination, and margins. I kept the papers but allowed students to take their bibliography pages home to redo. The second day was spent checking documentation and quotations for both form and completeness. On the third day students addressed grammar and mechanics before making corrections on their own papers.

At first the students objected to marking on their papers, but I convinced them that I would not penalize them and that they would have a better final product. And they did. Thanks to the proofreading, editing, and correcting done by the students before I received the papers, only a cursory glance at the bibliography and other documentation was necessary on my part. No more tedious examination of the location of periods, colons, and commas; no more time-consuming searches between internal citations and bibliography to see if they corresponded; no more hunting for the beginning and ending of quotations. I was able to devote my attention to the content of the paper.

Using clocking for the final exam proved even more successful. I first tried it in a one-semester composition course. We spent the week and a half preceding the exam period going through the stages of the writing process: prewriting, drafting, revising, and rewriting. The day of the exam students brought in their final products. The first hour was devoted to proofreading and making comments on editing sheets as students went "around the clock." In the remaining half hour students made corrections on their own papers.

For the first time in many years, I found I had a valid instrument for measuring what the students had learned. In addition, the quality of students' writing was higher, and because the papers contained far fewer errors, they required much less time to grade. I repeated the clocking procedure in all my classes during the next final exam period. While my colleagues frantically graded papers, averaged grades, and took care of the attendant paper work necessary at the end of the semester, I relaxed in the teachers' lounge, reading the latest best-seller, my work complete ahead of schedule.

Anne W. Tobias, Klein Forest High School, Houston, Texas

EASING INTO PEER EVALUATION

Introducing peer evaluation in a writing class can be a tricky maneuver; nevertheless, working with peer writers is a necessary part of a young writer's growth. My students enjoyed the following activity, which eases students into peer conferences while giving them insight into the writing process. The steps are as follows.

Begin by assigning a paper of two hundred to five hundred words. (The actual topic isn't important—almost any writing assignment could be used here.) Ask students to bring their rough drafts to class the next day for in-class revising. Before the next class period, cut enough 1" x 8½" paper strips for each student to have ten. The paper strips piled on your desk may raise questions, but let students wonder until you are ready to begin the activity.

Distribute ten strips to each student and ask students to transfer the first ten sentences from their rough drafts to the strips. Explain that they are to copy only one sentence per strip and that it's important *not* to number the sentences. This part of the activity will take about ten minutes. Next, each student shuffles his or her ten strips. Students then pair up and exchange their strips, and each one arranges the ten strips in what he or she feels is a logical sequence.

Since students don't know the original order of the sentences they receive, their sequences will usually vary from the original sequences at least a little, and often substantially. In the process of trying various arrangements, students consider meaning and sound and gain a sense for the alternatives writers have in composing. Point out that in rearranging sentences, there may not be "right" or "wrong" sequences, but that different sequences for the same sentences may have different meanings and that some sequences may make more sense or sound better to the reader.

Next, students meet with their partners to discuss and compare their arrangements of the sentences. (When I last used this activity, one student rearranged her sentences, met with her partner, and discovered that although she had reversed the original order exactly, both versions seemed to work equally well. Another student found that by changing the order, her partner had made the paragraph more forceful than the original. Still another student saw how switching the order of two sentences conveyed the same meaning but sounded more natural to the ear.)

After partners discuss their sentences, ask each student to select at random and revise one sentence from his or her partner's sequence of sentences. In isolating sentences from their context, students have a chance to analyze the merits of individual sentences without concern for context. These sentences and suggested revisions can then be discussed either in pairs or by the whole class. Questions to be considered might include the following:

> Is this sentence clear enough to be understood without the sentences before or after it?
> Could the order of the sentence parts be reversed for clearer meaning?
> Could any words be deleted or added to make this sentence stronger or more interesting?

Again at this stage, students see the value of making careful choices as they write and of getting feedback from other writers.

Kathleen Hebert, Metropolitan State College, Denver, Colorado

STOPLIGHT REVISION

Peer and teacher responders can be a valuable source of advice for student writers. "Stoplight Revision" is a way of facilitating communication between the writer and the reviewer. Students decide what their writings' strengths and weaknesses are—what parts they are proud of and what parts need work—and use the colors red (stop), yellow (caution), and green (go) to signal the reviewer as to the type of help they think they need.

Stop

Students use red pens or highlighters to designate passages or words that need to be examined by peer responders or the teacher and responded to with specific suggestions for changes. The red marking indicates that the writer definitely feels the need for help on this particular part of the composition; in addition, it forces the writer to identify the areas of greatest weakness in a meaningful type of self-evaluation. Writers using this mark are saying, "This part of my composition is bad and needs a lot of work. Where do you suggest that I begin?" (In the absence of markers, students may make minus marks.)

Caution

Students use yellow highlighters to designate passages or words that need to be examined by peer responders or the teacher and responded to with evaluative or analytical comments. The yellow marking indicates that the writer feels hesitant about this particular portion of the composition; it shows a willingness to receive comments directed at improvement from anyone who is willing to respond. Writers using this type of mark are essentially saying, "I know this is not as good as it could be. What can I do to make it better?" (In the absence of markers, students may make check marks.)

Go

Students use green pens or highlighters to designate passages or words that they feel have been well done. The green marking indicates that the writer feels good about this portion of the composition and wants to see if peer responders or the teacher agree; it assists the writer in recognizing particular strengths that may be utilized to advantage on compositions. Writers using this type of mark are saying, "I am proud of this part of my composition. Do you agree that I did a good job here?" (In the absence of markers, students may make plus marks.)

This method is effective because it allows students to make the important decisions about their writing, while providing them a simple way to request and accept advice from their peers.

Evelyn Alford, East Baton Rouge School System, Baton Rouge, Louisiana

STREAMLINING REVISIONS

Instead of you alone evaluating each paper your students write, why not share that evaluation process with the students? By offering other respondents to their writing you assist them in making their own revisions and decisions in the future. These techniques could be adapted for use at almost any grade level.

Pinup Papers

After collecting a batch of essays from your students, display the essays at eye level on bulletin boards or chalkboards around the classroom. Place them at least a foot apart to provide room for students to read. Then, give students fifteen or twenty minutes to get up from their desks and read as many papers as they can. I ask each student to mark at least one feature he or she likes in each paper, and one question or concern. This activity gives students more perspective on their writing.

Acted Out Assignments

At least once during the semester, assign students a writing project that lets students put the clarity of their writing to the test. Instruction papers are the best for this activity. Ask your students to explain to the class in writing how to do something simple: tie a shoe, put in contact lenses, tie a tie, etc. Test the quality of the instructions in class by asking other students to perform each procedure by strictly following written instructions from their classmates. Because procedures are evaluated according to standards of time and correct performance, make speed and accuracy your grading standards: the instructions that can be performed correctly the first time will receive the highest scores. I guarantee that your students will become excited about this assignment, and they will learn more about the importance of purpose, audience, organization, content, and precise word choice.

Just Say "Good"

Once in a while on at least one set of papers during the semester, force yourself to write positive comments only. When you see any sign of good work, mark it and explain why you like it. Your students will be happy to receive positive comments and will learn from them. Remember: praise is the best form of criticism.

Questions and Answers

When you assign an essay, also tell your students to write two or three questions in the margins of the final draft versions of their papers. Tell your students that the questions should focus on specific concerns they still have about their papers, even though their papers are in final draft form. Sample questions might include the following: Does my introduction interest you? Is my meaning clear here? Does this paragraph have enough convincing detail? Does this transition work here? Can you help me with this particular word?

Also indicate that for this assignment you will write no more than answers to their questions. Students will think more carefully about their writing and will be more receptive to comments and suggestions. You may use this approach to discover the unique and surprising ways students think about the process and the product of their writing.

I recommend that teachers use these time-saving approaches often, but not for every writing assignment during the term. We all know the importance of allowing students "in" on evaluation of writing and revising techniques. If you want students to assume more responsibility and interest in their writing, then consider using one of these approaches. Relinquish your role as the sole editor-in-chief of all classroom writing and delegate revision to your students, where it belongs.

Ned Williams, Brigham Young University—Hawaii Campus, Laie

| WORD SNAPSHOTS

Get your students published," echo presenters at professional conferences for English teachers. It sounds simple, but in a day-to-day routine that includes papers to be graded, the confines of curriculum, and faculty meetings to attend, many teachers end up putting off thoughts of a publication project "until next year."

"Next year" became "this year" for me and nine of my colleagues when we found a successful way to lead students into writing and informal publication: a "Word Snapshot" poetry unit. Word snapshots are poems of fifty words or less that recapture moments in students' lives. Because the assigned writings are short, students are less likely to feel intimidated. Final published form is a "photo album" that includes poems and accompanying illustrations.

To begin the unit, each teacher demonstrated the writing of a word snapshot and showed students a transparency of the poem and an illustration relating to the subject of the poem. The modeling was followed by a brainstorming session in which students listed important moments in their lives. After students spent a day or two writing about a variety of experiences ranging from school activities to memories of people close to them, they formed small groups for peer editing.

Peer editing groups received the following instructions:

1. Read the poem. In one sentence tell what the author is describing.
2. Underline vivid verbs, adjectives, and nouns that help you "see" the moment.
3. Draw a wavy line under verbs, adjectives, and nouns that seem weak or unclear.
4. Does the title seem to fit the poem? If not, what title would you suggest?
5. Is the illustrated frame suitable? Why or why not?
6. Count the words.

Once students had revised their word snapshots and submitted their final versions, all poems were displayed around the room for review by the whole class. My colleagues and I had decided that the published album would be a compilation of the best three poems from each class. A vote in each class determined their favorite three. (In a couple of cases, teachers found it necessary to override a class choice; however, this was done only where a poem's language or theme showed extremely poor taste.)

Poems were typed by a volunteer staff member, and teachers returned copies of the poems to the student authors for illustration. (Students whose poems were not chosen for inclusion in the album were still encouraged to illustrate their work and display it in the classroom.) We asked students to use black felt-tip pens for the purposes of mimeograph reproduction. The illustrated word snapshots were then cut, pasted, and photocopied two to a page in preparation for mimeographing.

Poems were arranged according to subject matter rather than class or level. The cover poem for the album was entitled "First Day," selected for the cover because it recalled students' initial high school fears. Because five of the poems focused on the deaths of the *Challenger* crew, the album was dedicated to the *Challenger* astronauts.

With students' help, the books were stapled together; larger compilations could be bound with plastic binders. The books were then distributed to students in all participating classrooms, and students immediately began passing around their albums for autographs and written good-byes on the inside covers.

Although our school district provides some funding for special projects, this project could be accomplished in any school district if teachers were careful to keep costs down. Selecting only three poems from each class was one way that my colleagues and I minimized expenses; another was to place two poems on each page, which not only saved paper costs but made the finished albums look more like real photo albums.

For those who haven't taken the plunge into "publishing," see how this project works for you. Don't rush it; allow yourself a semester to teach the unit, supervise revisions, and publish the albums. If you use this project on your own, you will probably want to include all student work in the final album. Last of all, remember to watch your students' faces for the pride and increased confidence that writing for publication can bring.

Rebecca B. Kutsko, Westfield High School, Houston, Texas

CRITIQUES WITHOUT TEARS

Critique of the student newspaper is necessary for its improvement, but for years I have been frustrated by typical staff critiques which caused resentment and defensiveness, and by attacks on students who had failed to turn in work, making them even less likely to turn in their next assignment. The full-class critique wasn't working.

We as a group needed to deepen the sense of teamwork while setting realistic, measurable goals for ourselves. Since I had recently attended my first cooperative learning workshop, I used the production of the first newspaper of the new school year as an opportunity to test a new technique. The emphasis this activity places on constructive critiques, self-analysis, and cooperative learning makes it adaptable to many other activities in the English classroom.

Its academic objectives are two-fold: (1) to analyze the content, form, and style of a student newspaper, and (2) to set measurable goals for improvement of the newspaper. But its social objective is the real benefit of this technique, and that objective is to criticize constructively without blaming, scapegoating, making excuses, or calling names.

The necessary materials are very basic: a copy of the student newspaper for each student, one critique sheet for each group (see page 140), one self-analysis sheet for each student (see page 140), and construction paper, markers, and tape.

Once we had our materials gathered, I divided the class into groups of three, making sure that each group had at least one first-year journalism student and one more-experienced student.

In each group, every student took on one of the following roles:

Recorder—to write critique responses
Monitor—to keep the group on-task and make sure the social objective is met
Encourager—to give positive feedback.

Each group selected one section or aspect of the newspaper to examine. These included photography, news coverage and writing, the opinions page, advertising, the sports page, and overall design. Students were asked to choose a section or aspect for which no one in the group was "professionally" responsible. For example, the group that included the opinions editor analyzed sports coverage, while the group that included the sports editor critiqued the opinions page.

After groups were set up, we were ready to explore critiquing behaviors. I wrote a "T" on the overhead, dividing the visual space into two separate sections. At the top of the T, I wrote the social objective. On the left side of the T, I wrote "Looks like," and on the right, "Sounds like." I asked the class to tell me what I would see or hear during a critiquing session, assuming that we were all making an effort to keep a positive attitude. For "Looks like," students suggested entries like "eye contact," "leaning closer to the person to listen to them," "not getting up while someone is talking," and "the group stays all together, facing one another." Sample "Sounds like" entries included "not talking while another person is talking," "using quiet voices," "using constructive words." After about four items were written on each side of the chart, the groups began orally analyzing the newspaper.

Groups were encouraged to establish *measurable* goals. A goal such as "more interesting pictures" might be changed to "all pictures should include at least one student." Goals should also be realistic. Even in the best student publications, a few typos can be expected, so cutting the number in half is a more realistic goal than "no typos." On the other hand, students should be challenged. The advertising group wrote that at least five people (out of a staff of nineteen) should sell ads. A better goal might have been to suggest that everyone on the staff sell at least one ad.

After groups wrote five goals on their critique sheets (section #6), they then were asked to write the three most important goals on construction paper and to place them on the wall. This provided the staff with a constant reminder of what they wanted to accomplish with the next publication. I asked each student to fill out a self-analysis form to measure student participation, group function, and effectiveness.

The second day, the groups reassembled to read their critiques and invite responses from the class. Students were much more careful to avoid blame and sarcasm than they had been in the whole-group sessions of the past. Almost without exception, the comments were positive, goal-oriented, and constructive. We put our "cry-rags" away and got to work on the next issue.

Cynthia Miller, Pflugerville High School, Pflugerville, Texas

Handout Page

Newspaper Critique

Group Members: _____   Date: _____

Area of newspaper to critique:

Write specific, complete answers to the following questions.

1. What are the three best things about this aspect of the newspaper?

   A.

   B.

   C.

2. What are the three things that most need to be improved?

   A.

   B.

   C.

3. What are some things that can be done to serve our readers better?

4. What are some ideas that will make the paper more visually appealing?

5. Rate the following aspects of your area, with 1 being best and 5 being worst.

Visual Impact	1	2	3	4	5	Not Applicable
Proofreading	1	2	3	4	5	Not Applicable
Interest	1	2	3	4	5	Not Applicable
Completeness	1	2	3	4	5	Not Applicable
Accuracy	1	2	3	4	5	Not Applicable
Ease of Understanding	1	2	3	4	5	Not Applicable

6. List five specific, reasonable goals for the next issue. Goals should be measurable and realistic.

Cooperative Learning Self-Analysis

Name: _____   Date: _____

I ...

1. listened to everyone without interrupting.   Yes   No
2. encouraged others to give ideas.   Yes   No
3. kept to the subject at hand.   Yes   No
4. felt I was listened to.   Yes   No
5. avoided talking to those in other groups.   Yes   No

My group:

1. gave equal time to all group members.   Yes   No
2. learned from one another.   Yes   No
3. followed the procedure.   Yes   No
4. criticized without put-downs.   Yes   No
5. avoided placing blame and making excuses.   Yes   No

I thought the educational objective was: Important   Not Important   Don't Know

I thought the social objective was: Important   Not Important   Don't Know

I think this activity was worth: Less Time   More Time   Just Right Amount

Do you feel you had a better chance to give your ideas than in a full-group critique, a worse chance, or did it matter at all? Please comment.

Please tell me what you learned from this activity, and what you would have liked to learn but didn't.

PLEASE VOTE: What was the best story of the issue, and why?

LET YOUR FINGERS DO THE WALKING . . .

N o matter how much I encourage my students to engage in peer conferencing as they revise and rethink their written work, they are still reluctant to consult their peers for help. I finally found a way to motivate students to consult one another, with what I call my "Yellow Pages" method.

After students have completed the first drafts of an assigned writing, I write on the chalkboard the following category headings: Coherence, Spelling/Punctuation, Organization, Clarity, Interest Level, Questions. We talk a little about what each of these words means in terms of judging a piece of writing. Then I tell students that they are going to be using the categories on the board as a "Yellow Pages Directory" of assistance as they revise their writings. Each student signs up in one category and is then available to the other students as a consultant in that area. I encourage students to sign up under what they consider "their area of expertise." To make sure that all the categories have more or less the same number of experts, I "close" a category when it has five or six signatures.

Before student writers begin work on their second drafts, they must obtain the signature of one expert from each category. A "Clarity Expert" reads the draft and makes comments and suggestions only on the clarity of the writing. A "Spelling/Punctuation Expert" looks only for misspelled words or faulty punctuation, and so on. In the "Questions" category, the student expert's task is simply to ask questions—"Why would Billy do such a thing?" "What happened after your parents found out?" "How could the car have gotten there without anyone hearing it?" These questions show the author of the draft which parts are unclear or need work and what details may be necessary to make the writing more interesting. I often take part in the activity myself by signing up under the category that has the least number of signatures and circulating my own rough draft through the "experts."

This activity allows every student to feel like an expert in one aspect of revision and accustoms students to having their writing read by others. By the time students obtain signatures in all categories, they have a wide range of reader feedback and are ready to begin revising.

John Harmon, APW High School, Parish, New York

"DEAR ME"

D ear Me" doesn't have to be a lament; it may instead be the beginning of an exercise that encourages students to evaluate their own writing and to set goals for themselves. At the midpoint or end of an English course, I ask students to spend one class period examining all the writings they have done in the previous months (drafts and final versions of essays, expository writings, and creative writings). With their writings before them, students are to complete the following letter to themselves. I ask them to be as thorough as they can in responding to the four topics.

> Dear Me,
> I've just looked over our writings, and I want to share my findings and feelings. Specifically, I'd like to share:
>
> 1. My overall impression
> 2. What parts I feel show good, strong writing
> 3. What parts I feel show weak writing
> 4. What I think we need to work on (What goals should we have for improving our writing?)
> Sincerely,

The resulting letters can be used in discussion or, if the exercise is used midyear, stored in a safe place so that students can refer to them later in the year. No matter when this exercise is used, student writers are bound to benefit by looking at their own work with a critical eye.

Roberta Young, Spring Woods High School, Houston, Texas